COMMON SENSE

YOUR Guide to Making Smart Choices with YOUR Money

By BRIAN SKROBONJA

Table of Contents

Acknowledgments

A person's beliefs, thoughts and actions are a result of the many experiences and relationships they have throughout their life. They help formulate the ideas and behavior of a person.

There are many people in my life who have fulfilled that role for me and who have encouraged and supported me in writing this book. They have contributed to and have inspired me to create Common Sense.

I want to thank my best friend and wife Kari, my awesome children Tyler, Malori and Hannah, my very supportive parents Branko and Debbie and my business coach Mike Lindstrom.

Thank you for your support and encouragement!

Foreword

A while back, I had a meeting with a couple who were beginning to think about retirement. They shared with me that they had worked their entire life to accumulate the money they had and wanted to take the necessary steps to preserve it for their retirement, and for their family after they were gone. During this meeting, the following questions arose:

- What do you think of the allocation that my advisor has suggested?
- How much money do I need to retire?
- How do I take the money that I have and begin drawing income for retirement?
- What if I lose money in the market?
- Will I have enough money to retire on?

I have had hundreds of similar conversations over the years, where clients ask dozens of questions about their money, questions which I feel should have been answered by their financial advisors. However, it seems that the only thing being offered by these advisors is confusion.

What I have determined to be true is that most advisors leave their clients insecure about their investment portfolio, unprepared for retirement, and disoriented about their options. This is what motivated me to write this book. I want to set the record straight—financial planning is not simply the purchase of a product. It is a mindset for how to position and use the money you have.

Money and investing are not complicated, but they seem that way, because many financial professionals are ill-equipped to provide clear, comprehensible financial coaching. They are trained to sell products, not to solve problems, and this has created a vacuum of leadership for assisting the public with making important financial decisions. This vacuum leaves many people unaware of what is available to them beyond simply buying an investment product. This trend needs to be stopped to help reduce the lack of confidence I see in new clients, and to eliminate the mindset that financial planning is cumbersome and difficult to understand.

When I sat down to write this book, I thought hard about what I wanted people to walk away with after reading it. Creating a book that can help readers overcome the most common financial-planning struggles is a fairly large proposition. I thought about what I could offer people that would impact their lives in a positive way and empower them with the right mindset about money. I knew that if people could walk away from reading this book with a new skill set, one that would enable them to make smart choices with their money, then I would have accomplished something that very few books on finance have successfully done.

However, I realized right away that in order for this book to fulfill what I have set out to do, readers would need to open their mind to new ideas and a new way of thinking about their money. There is so much noise in the media about what you should and shouldn't do that many people have a corrupt mental perception about financial planning. So I knew that in order for this book to accomplish its intended purpose, readers would need to hit the reset button and allow themselves to reprogram their view of financial planning.

The best way for me to explain is to say this: what you have done in the past has gotten you to where you are today, and what you are doing today may very well keep you where you are at. In other words, you have to change what you are doing in order for change to occur.

You can apply this to any area of your life. Look at your marriage. Look at your relationships with friends and family. Look at your finances. They all have a common denominator, and it is that where you are today is a direct result of the behavior and actions you have taken until this point. So it only makes sense that if we want something to improve, then we must change what we are doing to create a better result.

For years I have taught that achieving your finance goals is more about doing the right things on a regular basis, and less about rate of return on your investments. This philosophy has helped many of my clients create a mindset for financial planning, and a way of thinking that allows them to incorporate successful strategies for maximizing the use of their money.

Taking the strategies described in this book and applying them to your daily life begins with an understanding of what steps you need to take to get there. It involves knowing what you should be doing, and then doing it. We all have a list in our head that includes things that we *should* be doing, actions we *should* be taking and preventative steps we *should* consider to better our situation. It is our *Should List.*

When it comes to financial planning, your *Should List* may include things such as these:

- I really should get a will in place.
- I really should shop our insurance for better rates and coverage.
- I really should review our investment allocations to see how they compare to other options.
- I really should investigate mortgage rates while they are low.
- I really should gather my tax information for a year-end check.

Your list may also include things like:

- I really should exercise.
- I really should read more.
- I really should...*fill in the blank.*

Now, imagine for a moment that you were to take action on everything on your list. Imagine for the moment that everything has been satisfied. What would that look like for you? How different would your life be? How much less stress would you have in your life? Now the question is this: what's stopping you from doing it?

This book will lead you through creating a mindset for making smart choices with your money. I am hopeful that you find a new level of awareness about money and a new way of thinking that will help you take your money to the next level.

CHAPTER ONE

Next Level Thinking

It is said that the most difficult relationships people have are with their personal self-image, and with their money. This may not be the case with everyone, but it certainly hits the nail on the head for the rest of us. According to a January 2009 *Forbes* article, Americans spent $11 billion in 2008 on self-improvement books. That is a lot of books!

Think about the number of exercise and weight-loss programs you see advertised. How about the get-rich-quick schemes by financial gurus promising the moon? Our insecurities are driving an enormous market for "experts" to provide the answers we are seeking. However, if they are truly offering solutions to our problems, then why is the industry growing? A few books should do the trick—right?

The reality is that to lose weight, you must take in fewer calories than you burn, and to have money, you must spend less than you earn.

It is really that simple isn't it? We know we have to eat less and spend less to get the outcome we desire. This is easier to say than to do, of course, and it takes hard work and commitment to get the results we want.

The biggest obstacle to achieving our goals is ourselves. It is that continual conversation we have with our inner self that convinces us that we cannot do something, or that it is too difficult.

In order for any of us to get to where we want to be, we have to overcome the idea that the next level is too far out of reach, or that getting there is too difficult and confusing. To get to the next level, you have to adopt new ways of thinking and incorporate new ideas into what you are doing with your money.

Let me ask you a question. When was the last time you actually stopped to consider the process you use to make a decision? If you were able to identify the one thing that drives your decision-making, and if you could articulate your beliefs about how you do it, what would it be? This is difficult, because the truth of the matter is, most decisions are made at a subconscious level, but if you had to come up with an answer, what is the "switch" in your head that drives the decision?

This "switch" is likely different from one person to the next, but the process for how we arrive at a decision is the same, and here it is: we have all had experiences (events or circumstances) in our life that have molded our belief system (how we view things), which is what drives our behavior (actions and decision-making), which is what creates our outcome (results in life).

Think about it. Every day, you experience things that mold you into who you are, and when you have to make a decision, you draw from those past experiences, and the decision you make creates an outcome or a result in your life. This is the "switch," and it is happening every day to you on a subconscious level.

Why am I explaining this, and what does this have to do with money?

People struggle every day with identifying why they are getting the results they are getting, or why they are in the position they are in. Think about the last time you asked yourself such a question. "Why am I struggling in my marriage?. Why am I struggling with my finances? Why am I having a difficult time with my relationships? Why am I…*fill in the blank*? There is always that question of why something is happening, with little understanding about how to fix it.

The beginning of the solution for creating change in your life is to understand that in order to experience change, you have to first change your attitude and your belief system. If you keep doing what you have always done, you will continue to get the same outcome.

Let me give you an example using something parents do all the time with their kids. A child says, "I cannot do this." The parent says, "Yes, you can." And then with some effort, the kid does what he thought could not be done. At first, the child had a belief that he could not do it, but the parent helped him experience success, and now the child believes that he can do it. Now, when this task is presented to this same child in the future, he knows he can do it, because he has accomplished it before. This same principal can be used for you, and can be applied to almost anything, including your finances.

Assume for illustrative purposes that where you are now is not where you want to be financially. First of all, understand that everything you have been doing has gotten you to where you are now, and that what you have been doing will also keep you where you are now. Simply put, you cannot continue to do the same things and expect different results.

Second, understand that there is a level of discomfort when changes are made. While you are reprogramming yourself to do things differently, it may feel a bit uncomfortable or somewhat odd. In this book, I will walk you through a different way of thinking about money and help you create a "switch" which will help better equip you in your financial decision-making the rest of your financial life.

In this book, I will take you through an easy-to-follow process for creating a new level of financial awareness. During my years of experience helping people like you, I have identified the most common planning mistakes people make, and here I will provide solutions for how to avoid them.

What I know to be true is that you more than likely fall into one of the five following financial life stages:

- Developing a Financial Footing
- Building Assets for Future Use
- Protecting Assets from Inflation and Market Losses
- Distributing Assets for Income
- Transferring Assets to Heirs

We will cover all of these categories in the coming chapters and offer common questions and answers for how to work through planning your financial future, regardless of what stage you are presently in.

Before we get started, let me congratulate you for taking the time to read this book. By carving out time to invest in yourself, you are showing a commitment to making smart choices with your money, as well as a desire to get the most from what you have. I am certain that when you finish reading this book, you will feel energized, confident, and eager to ask yourself great questions that will help shape your financial future.

CHAPTER TWO

Keeping up with the Joneses

We have all heard the proverbial fish story, where each time the story is told, the fish that was caught gets bigger and bigger. Why does the fish grow bigger every time the story is told? I believe it is to hook you into listening to the story, and to make the fisherman out to be better or more skillful than the next person. A five-pound fish is not that interesting, but a twenty-pound fish… well, that is impressive! It is a way to impress and grab attention.

It is probably not a big deal when you are listening to a story about a fish, but what if a friend is telling you a fish story about his money? How does that affect how you view your own financial position?

For example, a friend tells you that she just paid off her home. How do you interpret that? I contend that you would immediately begin to evaluate her financial situation. Perhaps you know what she does for a living, the size of the home she has, the kind of car she drives, the number of kids she has, and so on. You calculate in your mind what her financial picture looks like, comparing it to your own situation. Then you determine that she must know something you don't, because your situations are similar, and there is no way you could pay off your home. So how did she manage that? In other words, was the fish really that big, or is the story embellished to impress you?

This is your cue to take a time out. Before you allow feelings of jealousy or even depression over what your friend has done creep into your life, take a deep breath and realize that there is more than likely information missing in this equation. There is no magic wand or secret process for getting ahead financially. Perhaps your friend did not mention a gift she received from a parent, which enabled her to pay her home off. Now that changes things, doesn't it?

Since money is a measurement of status, it may explain why a friend may not tell you how she paid the home off, but she still wants you to know that she did it. Telling you how she did it may make it seem less of an accomplishment, so leaving this part out makes it appear to be a big deal. Whether you call that deception or vanity, it is what it is.

So why am I talking about this? Over the years, I have had many clients struggle with what I call their financial identity. They are disoriented by what they hear and see other people doing, and they want to know where they should be for their age and situation. To help articulate this issue, it is important to point out why they are feeling this way, and it begins with understanding that what you see is not always a true reflection of someone's financial situation. At the end of the day, I believe this has everything to do with the "keeping up with the Joneses" syndrome, and it is a slippery slope, since you will never know the whole story. Instead of comparing yourself to an imaginary twenty-pound fish, setting goals and planning out your spending each year based on what you have and know to be true will provide you with the best measurement for determining your success.

Comparing yourself to others will likely only lead to a feeling of frustration. Instead, make your money an area of your life managed against your own goals. Work to accomplish what is best for your family, and that will propel you toward contentment.

When you think about it, there are many different stereotypes about money. For instance, you may know people who are "frugal" with their money, while you may consider others "free-spending." Some you may view as "calculating," while others you see as "emotional." These are all opinions and stereotypes that we have formed about people's behavior with their money. You may look up to and have a positive perception of those you agree with, while looking down your nose at those whose views you do not admire.

Our beliefs about people and our own behavior with money illustrate how society and our experiences have led us to have a certain view of what is the "right" way to handle money, and what is the "wrong" way of handling money. However, it may surprise you to realize that your opinion of what is right does not mean that what others are doing is wrong. You do what you do, because of what someone taught you, or an experience that you had, while the same is true for others. There is not a single, correct way of handling money.

It is helpful to view money as a tool for providing something in your life. This helps you to shift your focus away from money itself, and more toward the things that mean the most to you. The question then becomes, what is most important to you?

What I have found to be true is that people tend to hold one of the two following beliefs about money:

1. Money is something you accumulate and hold onto. It is something that is preserved, and the goal is to have a lot of it. Money itself is the goal.
2. Money is something used to acquire things. It is a means to live your life. Money is not the goal; what the money can buy is the goal.

Here are two very simple illustrations of how these differing views may look:

1. A retiree has lived in the same house for forty years with a million dollars sitting in a bank, while he lives off of Social Security and a pension. He never uses the money in the bank for anything. All his needs are met. Life is good.
2. A retiree has a house on a lake, which he just bought. He keeps a few dollars in the bank for emergencies and lives comfortably off of Social Security and a pension. All his needs are met. Life is good.

Neither person is using his money better than the other. The example does not show that one man is better with money than the other. It simply shows that each man views money differently. So before you adopt someone else's way of thinking, let's walk through identifying what your purpose for money is.

When constructing a home, the first step in the process is a vision for what the home will look like. You envision the room sizes, brick color, landscaping, countertops, deck size, and the view from your window. You then take those ideas and share them with an architect, who figures out how to make your vision a reality. After the drawings are made and permits are pulled, construction begins, with qualified professionals capable of making the drawing a reality.

While this seems like common sense for building a home, this is also an apt metaphor for building a financial plan. Unfortunately many people—and even some financial advisors—do not understand this process. They treat buying an investment as if they were building a house by just buying a piece of land, having lumber delivered, and starting to nail that lumber together. They have no blueprints, no plan—just nails and lumber.

So how do we translate the process for building a home into building a financial plan? The answer is to begin with the end in mind.

Everyone who saves and accumulates money does so with the intent to use it at some point, for some purpose. Identifying the purpose for your money, and understanding how you will ultimately use it is the key to developing a successful financial plan.

When you think about it, money can be put into one of two categories:

- Money you will spend on big-ticket items such as cars, refrigerators (and other appliances), and education. In other words, the money will be spent in a lump sum.
- Money you will use as an income source for budget-related items in retirement. The principal will be preserved, while drawing income from its earnings.

My experience working with people who come into my office after having worked with another financial advisor is that they often have a portfolio of investments that does not align with what they are trying to do. The investments are not necessarily bad, but are often incongruent with their goals.

By starting with the end in mind, you can begin to construct a financial plan that will act as a blueprint for how to build your vision for the future, and which will ultimately offer guidance for how to arrange your investment portfolio.

Your current financial position will determine how you will approach the development of your plan. However, the principals and exercises within the following pages will offer guidance to anyone who wants to maximize the use of their money.

CHAPTER THREE

Life Phases

Have you ever questioned what you should be doing with your money? If you are like many other people who subscribe to newsletters and magazines, you are inundated with suggestions for how you should be investing and managing your money. It can be a bit overwhelming, and to make it worse, you are likely running on information overload, which can ultimately lead to paralysis.

The reality is that when people feel confused or unsure of what to do, they often do nothing, believing that this is the safest route. You cannot make a wrong decision if you make no decision, right? Unfortunately, it is necessary to sort through all of this information and make decisions that are best suited for what you are trying to accomplish, regardless of how you feel about it. Otherwise ten or twenty years from now, you will be in the same boat that you are in today, wishing you had done something to better your situation.

So what do you do when you have all of this information coming at you? How do you know what to do, and when to do it? The process involves creating mental filters that will help you to process information as it is coming at you. The filters will help you identify the information you need to consider for your situation and provide clarity about what needs to be ignored.

To begin, it is important to understand what phase of life you are in. In other words, what are the things in your life that have influence in how you define your financial priorities? This is the first step in creating your filter and is the conduit to eliminating the frustration that comes with financial planning.

Contrary to what most people may believe, your phase of life has less to do with your age and more to do with what you have going on in your life. For instance, if you are twenty-five with a new baby, you probably should not be overly concerned about your retirement plans right now. You have more pressing matters to contend with, such as establishing a family and covering your present financial needs.

There is no doubt that common sense should be a part of how you navigate through these phases, but keep in mind that identifying chronological needs is the driver for identifying what phase of life you are in, and what you should be considering as you transition from one phase to the next.

Phase One: Developing a Financial Footing

We all have to start somewhere, and this is where we begin. Developing a financial footing is important for shaping your future. You can think of this as your financial foundation, and how well you structure this determines how secure the rest of your financial planning is.

The focus for this phase is to cover your risk, build savings, and position yourself for the next level.

- Build short-term savings for emergencies. This would equal three to six months of your living expenses. A job loss or random setback may require you to live off of your savings until you get back on your feet. Not having adequate savings may create debt, which is something we are striving to avoid.
- Save for large purchases. Since you are just getting started, you may need to accumulate enough money to make a down payment on a home, or perhaps you have a desire to purchase a new automobile. Regardless of what the item is, it will require you to save money.
- Have adequate insurance coverage. We will cover these in length in a later chapter but these would include insurance for your auto, home, life, disability, and health. Passing the

risk of loss on to an insurance company is important, since any unforeseen incident can wipe you out financially and place a financial burden on you that could last a lifetime.

■ Formulate a spending plan for your income. It is imperative that your spending habits do not exceed your income, and that you incorporate your savings goals into your budget. This is the primary reason people accumulate credit card debt. They overlook the need to not only budget for reoccurring expenses, but also for the unforeseen expenses which surely will arise.

So if you are in this initial phase of life, then a good filter to use may be that if it does not have anything to do with covering your risks and building short-term savings, then you should probably avoid it for now.

Phase Two: Investing in Shelter and Education

As you enter into a life of responsibilities, you soon experience the pressures of making ends meet as your expenses increase with the rising cost of raising a family and maintaining a home. This is a phase of life that if you are not careful can lead to credit card debt as expenses exceed income.

The good news is that if you have successfully established the previous phase, you are well-equipped to work through these added pressures and to continue working toward this next level, which is the entry into investing and debt avoidance. In this phase of life, you will want to consider the following:

1. Are you renting, or do you own a home? Now that you have your risks covered and savings established, it is time to begin investing in your future, which includes real estate. If you have not already done so, you may want to consider the purchase of a home.

2. If you have children, their college education is a large financial obligation that you know is imminent. The biggest challenge many parents face is whether they should save for their child's education, or save for their retirement. Often, depending on your financial situation, saving for both can leave you short of both goals. If you find yourself wondering which one to save for, the answer is simple: save for retirement! The logic here is that your child can borrow money

for college, while you cannot borrow for retirement. It is not advisable to put your retirement at risk to cover tuition bills. If you do plan to cover this expense for your children, you need to begin saving now.

As you can see, this phase brings to life the need to think long-term. Your filter for this phase is owning a home, setting a five to ten year goal for investing, and if desired, saving for a child's education. Anything outside of this needs to be postponed until you get this phase ironed out.

Phase Three: Investing in Your Retirement

Now that you have graduated from the basics, you are now ready to move into long-term investments. Keep in mind that this phase has to do with money you will not use until you are retired from work. It is not money you will have easy access to, which is why the previous phases are critically important.

A word of caution here is that you should not choose a savings account simply because of a tax deduction. This is a common trap that people jump into head first, and this is not the proper filter to use when saving your money for future use. A good question to ask yourself before jumping into a tax-deductible account is this: "Am I avoiding taxes, or am I simply deferring taxes?" If you are simply avoiding taxes today, you will pay them later when you plan to use the money.

So, where is the advantage? Today, you have the child tax credit and mortgage interest to deduct, which will help you offset some tax liability, but these deductions may not be available when you retire, leaving the money you deferred exposed to potentially higher tax liabilities. You must also consider the fact that tax rates are likely to rise...not go down. I will explain this more in coming chapters, but for now, let's focus on where to put your money for retirement purposes.

1. Your employer's 401k is an option, assuming that there is a match. If there is not a match, then I would not contribute to this plan.
2. A Roth IRA may be an option since the money grows tax-free and can be withdrawn tax-free. If your income is above the threshold for eligibility, prompt your employer to offer a

Roth 401k, or you can contribute to a traditional IRA, then convert it to a Roth IRA a bit later.

3. If you are not eligible for a Roth IRA or a traditional IRA, and your employer is not offering a Roth 401k, municipal bonds or an investment-grade life insurance policy are alternatives for tax-free access to your money.

So the filter to use when saving for retirement is how the money will be used, not how the money will be saved. The tax deduction is not as important as the tax liability you will have when withdrawing the money.

Phase Four: Distributing Assets for Retirement Income

If you are approaching retirement or have already retired, how you position your money will determine the longevity of your retirement resources, as well as your quality of life. Saving money is the easy part. Protecting the money and distributing it for income purposes is a bit more complicated.

If you are a risk-taker and feel the markets will continue to climb in perpetuity, then keeping your money in traditional investments is probably OK for you. Just keep in mind that your sense of confidence does not remove the risk associated with investing. There is still the chance of losing money, which could necessarily cause your income to decrease in retirement.

I tend to believe that guarantees when planning for retirement income are a good policy, since the markets are unpredictable, and your income depends on consistency. My focus would be to protect the purpose of the money, and that purpose is clearly income. I will discuss this more in my retirement income chapter.

The balance of the money, which you may not need for income today, may be needed later to supplement your income due to inflation or added expenses. This money needs to be focused on growth, with an emphasis on preservation.

Your filter here is determined by the use of the money. If the purpose is income now, look to possible investments that offer you the protection you need to guarantee the income you desire. If the money is for use down the road, then look to the option that preserves your principal, while attempting to grow income for later.

Phase Five: Transferring to the Next Generation

Now that you have fulfilled your life goals and are planning to pass what you have onto the next generation, you will want to make the most of what you have worked a lifetime to accumulate. I will jump right into a few of the most important aspects to passing your estate onto your family.

1. The use of a will or a trust is important to communicate to your family members what your wishes are and can help to preserve family unity.
2. If you have money that you are not using, and your health is good, the use of life insurance is a guaranteed way to double or even triple the amount of money you pass along to your heirs, and the death proceeds from a life insurance policy are tax-free.
3. A beneficiary review is a good idea to verify that the account or assets are correctly designated. If you have a trust, make sure the appropriate assets are titled to the trust. This includes titles to homes and bank accounts. An attorney can assist in making sure this is done correctly.

The filter for this phase of life should be focused on how the money will be used, not how the money is being stored. In other words, the question to ask is, "What is the maximum benefit to be received by your heirs?" This may be very different from how you position the money you need or are using to live on.

The biggest challenge I see is with the mindset some people possess that all their money should be managed in the same manner. This is appropriate if all your money is for the same purpose, but this is seldom the case. The key to maximizing your money is understanding what you are trying to accomplish and identifying how the money will be used.

— CHAPTER FOUR —

Getting Started

One of the most challenging aspects of money management for the average person is the accountability of how it is used. Busy lifestyles and poor habits leave little time for us to properly manage our hard-earned money. It often becomes a cycle of addressing problems as they arise, and otherwise sinking into an *out of sight, out of mind* mindset.

For some, the idea of managing money is that it is an unnecessary task, as long as there is money in the bank. The truth of the matter is you can get away with not having a spending plan for your money—simply do not allow your spending to exceed your income. It really is that simple. However, the point of this entire book is to show you how to do more than to simply get by. It is about getting to the next level financially, and in order to accomplish this task, you absolutely have to start by completing a cash flow awareness exercise. It truly is not possible without it. You can download a cash flow awareness worksheet on my website at www.skrobonjafinancialgroup.com.

Before we get too far, I want to say that money should be *managed*, whether you have an abundance of cash on hand, or whether you live paycheck to paycheck. A common misconception I hear is that those who are well off have no need to track spending. The truth of the matter is that managing cash flow can help everyone, in all economic classes, get to the next level financially. The difference is that the more money you make, the bigger the mistakes you make.

You have to know two things in order to make progress with anything you are doing: you have to know where you are, and you have to know where you are going. The reality for most people is that money seems to come into our lives, but quickly leaves month after month and year after year, and people have little understanding of where the money goes and how it is spent. It does not have to be that way, and you do not need an accounting degree or a sick fascination with numbers and spreadsheets to track your cash flow.

The purpose behind cash flow awareness is not to make ends meet, but rather to properly organize your money, which allows you to create wealth, and avoid debt. It is a fairly straightforward process, which need not take a lot of time if you follow a few basic steps:

1. Instead of viewing your checkbook as a means to pay bills, view your household as a profit center. This means that you run your household like a business, with the goal of being profitable, in lieu of just making it through another month.
2. Treat yourself as the Chief Financial Officer of your household, with the responsibility for making a profit. At year end, you need to be able to answer questions like these:

    -   How much income did you earn?
    -   How much in taxes did you pay?
    -   How much money did you spend?
    -   How much profit did you make?

3. Understand that in order for you to determine profitability, you must start by determining where you are.

    -   Are you running in the red or in the black?
    -   What are your current income and expenses?
    -   What comes out of your paycheck automatically?

4. Create a system for tracking your income and expenses going forward.

    -   Utilize an accounting software program to track your spending.

- Enter your transactions, creating specific categories.
- After a full quarter of using the program, run a report and average the results. Then compare it to your self-assessment from step three (above).
- If there is a negative number, identify wasteful spending or optional expenditures, and remove those expenses from your budget. If there is a positive number, increase the line item for savings.
- Repeat the process listed above for four consecutive quarters. Then make it part of your annual financial planning review.

This may require you to change how you have always done things, but it can make a difference, and believe it or not, it may even make your life easier. A budget is a key component for creating a true sense of where you are and is the nucleus of your financial plan.

Once you have established the exercise, you will see that your planned spending ties directly into the goals you defined in a previous chapter. As you read this book, you will begin to see how all the different areas of your financial life are dependent on the next to make the financial plan a viable tool for your financial success.

When I work with a new client, the primary goal I have is to help her define with crystal clarity the purpose of the money she has, and how she plans to use it. The same is true for you as you read this book. Defining your intention for the money you have, or will accumulate, allows you to begin to assemble your financial plan in a strategic, chronological manner.

The first step in this process is identifying when the money will be used. I would recommend you take some time and begin writing out your short-term goals, which may include anything you need money for within the next two to five years. This should include money designated for emergencies, home repairs, furniture, or a new car. The defining purpose of this money would be categorized as money you will spend.

Once you have a very clear outline of your short-term needs, take your vision a little further down the road and begin thinking about your medium-term goals. This would include anything you are wanting money for within a time frame of roughly five to twenty years, or leading up to retirement. This should include things such as a new home or financing a child's education, perhaps taking a dream vacation, or starting the business you have always wanted to open. The defining purpose of this money would also be categorized as money you will spend.

Finally, list your long-term goals. This would include such things as retirement. This is often a category where you acknowledge that the purpose of the money is for income generation and will be used to support your living expenses and other budgetary needs.

The purpose of this process is to help you visualize and define what you want to accomplish, and when you will need your money. It is a chronological road map for your finances and will serve as a compass when making a financial decision. When making a purchase or investment decision, referring to this schematic of your short, medium and long-term goals will assist you in recognizing what is most suitable.

Another critical aspect of this process is that you are defining how you will use the money. You will either use the principal of the money as a lump sum to make a purchase, as defined in your goals, or you will use the money as a source of income for retirement to supplement your budgetary needs.

Unfortunately, this is an area many financial advisors miss, as they often handle all money the same, which can be a detriment to maximizing the use of the money. In my opinion, this occurs because most financial advisors are solely focused on investments and are not considering the financial-planning needs of their clients.

The next step is to develop a list of your current investments, savings accounts, and other assets, and to begin to develop a purpose for your money that is congruent with your goals. Begin this process by breaking down your accounts and assets by owner. If you are a husband and wife, create separate lists, and make joint accounts a third category. Then, you will want to break the list down further by separating the money into qualified and non-qualified assets. (Qualified means that it is a government-sponsored program such as an IRA or 401k. Non-qualified means that it is not qualified.)

Once you complete these lists, begin to identify when the money will be used and then insert dollar amounts from your current assets. (It is helpful to draw out three columns on a piece of paper, labeled short-, medium-, and long-term.) During this process, you may recognize that this approach will require you to adjust how you are currently viewing your money. This is a good sign that you are aligning your money with your financial goals.

If the money is qualified, it will more than likely be immediately categorized as long-term, to be used for income. If the money is non-qualified, it will likely be used for short- and medium-term purposes, in combination with the one to six months of budget requirements to act as a "Rainy Day Fund."

You may find as you go through this process that you have either run out of assets to categorize, or you will have money left over. If you find yourself with money left over, consider adding a fourth column labeled Legacy, which will be used to benefit your family and favorite charities. We will cover this in a later chapter.

If you are just getting started and do not have assets to move around, begin identifying money within your budget that you can save monthly, noting that in the short-term category. Once you have adequate savings in this category, move on to the next, and so on.

— CHAPTER FIVE —

Protecting Your Assets

When we think of our most important assets relating to personal financial planning, we typically think of such things as our home, our savings, a retirement account, or other investments. For most people, these assets make up most of our financial self-worth and are designed to fill a specified purpose or event at some future time. However, when you think about it, our largest asset is really our ability to earn an income. If you take your salary and multiply it by the number of years you plan to work, this is likely a larger number than any of the other assets listed.

The goal for this chapter is to get you thinking about the things that you have no control over. It is relatively easy to sit and think through the amount of money you will save over ten, twenty, or thirty years, but what if something happens that you have not planned for? The truth is that when we sit and think of the future, we envision successful events and happy times with family and friends. Very seldom do we daydream about an early death or some other circumstance that may affect our long-term outlook. Whatever you are dreaming about for the future, I recommend planning for different scenarios since we do not know what the future truly holds for us.

It is advisable to prepare for the worst and hope for the best while planning your future. This approach gives you the flexibility to work toward your goals while covering your risks. The fact is that there are unforeseen circumstances that could affect your family and your long-term plans. A sickness or deadly accident can leave a family emotionally and financially devastated. If you do not think that can happen to you, take a look around, and it won't take long for you to see family after family where injury, disease, or an accident has affected their life.

So ask yourself, how are you doing in this area? Do you feel like you have your bases covered, or are you kicking the can down the road, unwilling to address these matters? Do you have a plan for covering these types of scenarios, or do you have a superman syndrome?

What I have found to be true is that the vast majority of people have done very little to protect themselves and their families from an unforeseen death or illness. Many shrug this off, saying, "I will take care of this later," or "We have this taken care of through work." The reality is that later never comes, and your work is unable to provide you with the education and benefits you need to protect your income.

The scenarios are endless, but consider this: what if you and your spouse are both taken from your kids? How will they be cared for financially, and who will provide for their well-being? Some would say, "We have this covered. They will go to my brother or sister." That's a great idea, but can that sister or brother afford to take on one, two, or three kids without some financial assistance? The truth is that most families are dependent on their entire income, making them vulnerable to financial devastation if an illness, injury, or death occurs.

To develop a financial plan without gaps or omissions, it is important for us to take a serious look at how these issues could affect your family financially.

Life Insurance

If you make $3,000 per month, and your spouse makes the same, you have a monthly cash flow of $6,000. If one or the other of you should die, or grow too ill to work, then your income is cut in half. That means your house payment, food, clothing—everything is cut in half immediately! What is your plan to cover this? If you are a one-income family, you go from $6,000 per month to nothing, immediately! What steps have you taken to protect your family from this situation?

Consider your current income compounded with inflation over the next ten, twenty, thirty years, coupled with company benefits, and you can see that your actual monetary value over your lifetime can be fairly substantial, making your ability to work the largest asset you have.

To replace $36,000 per year of income after a death would take nearly three-quarters of a million dollars. This does not include pay increases or any company-provided health insurance, only the income received. To replace $72,000 would take twice that—approximately a million and a half dollars. (The math for this is simple: divide your income by a presumed interest rate, say five percent: $36,000 divided by 0.05 = $740,000; or $72,000 divided by 0.05 = $1,440,000.)

So in that scenario, if you or your spouse dies, how do you create hundreds of thousands of dollars overnight? The answer is through the use of life insurance. Life insurance is a contract that pays a sum of money to surviving family members when a death occurs.

Another common effect of life insurance is to protect a spouse in retirement. If you have enough assets after you retire, the income for a surviving spouse may be sufficient to maintain a reasonable lifestyle. However, for a couple dependent on current income or a pension to make ends meet, an early death will negatively affect the financial position of the surviving spouse. The long-term plans you had for your assets may no longer be possible, and the surviving spouse may even need to sell off accumulated assets to pay bills.

It's important to note that while insurance proceeds are not taxable, the earnings on the income will be. So when calculating income payments from the proceeds, be sure to include tax obligations, just as you would if you were working.

Disability

Financially, an illness can be worse than a death, when you consider medical bills and the possibility that the other spouse might need to miss work to care for the sick spouse. This type of coverage is often provided by an employer, but keep in mind that this is a fairly complex form of insurance and feeling confident that you are covered is not as easy as simply stating, "I have something through work." Coverage through work can often carry caveats, such as having to be hurt on the job, or it may only cover you for a short period of time, while other plans are very comprehensive and adequate to cover your needs. My point is that you should know with certainty how your coverage works.

In addition, taxes are a big consideration when determining how much coverage you should carry. Proceeds from a disability program are taxable if your employer paid all of the disability premiums, and did not include the amount in your gross income. On the other hand, if you paid all of the premiums with after-tax income, your benefits should be exempt from tax.

So, if you have a taxable benefit that covers sixty percent of your income, you could be looking at a significant chasm between what you were earning and what your benefit amount is. It would be advisable to clarify whether your plan is taxable or tax-free.

Long-Term Care

There may come a time in your life when you require skilled nursing assistance to help perform daily activities such as bathing, eating, dressing etc. It is not something any of us want to think about for our golden years, but it is something to plan for.

I will not get into the technical aspects of long-term care planning due to its complexities and the many variables associated with it. However, we will cover what you should think about and help you find some direction for understanding its use.

As with all forms of insurance, the first thing is to evaluate whether or not you need coverage. In other words, what is at risk? What are you insuring? After all, there is no need for coverage, if there is no risk of loss.

The core need for long-term care insurance from a financial planning perspective is to help protect personal assets from being eroded by the ever-increasing cost of care. A nursing home facility can cost upwards of $200 or $300 per day, and can quickly exhaust an investment portfolio, leaving a healthy spouse in a difficult financial situation. So, if you are married and have a fair amount of assets, you may want to take a careful look at long-term care insurance coverage.

A unique consideration for long-term care is the situation when an unnecessary burden is placed onto someone you love who lacks the means to cover the time and expenses involved. If you know someone who has cared for a loved one, you know that it is not something most of us want to do to someone we care about. The stress involved, as well as the loss of personal income from being away from a job is cause enough for making arrangements if this were to happen to you. The most economical approach is through the use of long-term care insurance.

With that said, if you do not have much in savings and investments, then I would tend to put off spending money on insurance. Unfortunately, it is not always possible to pay the premiums for such coverage. If someone is struggling to save for retirement, she may want this type of coverage, but it may not be the best use of her income. In this case, there are government programs available, such as Medicaid for those who have little or no assets, but who require skilled care in a nursing home.

There are other forms of insurance as well, such as health, automobile, and home, all of which you should be evaluating annually to determine your best options for the next year. Just be sure to not only compare pricing for this type of insurance, but also to verify that your coverage is adequate to meet your needs and cover your risk.

Keep in mind that the purpose behind this book is to help you develop filters for what to look for. Each chapter in this book could be a book in and of itself, and each topic is so complex that it nearly impossible for me to take a truly in-depth look into each subject. I encourage you to call or email my office with questions should you require more information, at 636-296-5225.

The bottom line when it comes to insurance is that you must realize that you are protecting your family's finances and well-being. This responsibility should not be taken lightly, otherwise you may very well be putting your family in a bad situation. Take the time to plan accordingly, and do not overlook the need for adequate insurance coverage.

CHAPTER SIX

Life Insurance

The use of life insurance is so widely debated that I thought it warranted its own chapter to discuss the many aspects of its use and how to view each type of policy. Knowing what type of policy to purchase, and how much insurance to carry is critical, as is knowing which will work best for your situation. The following will help equip you with the knowledge and information you need to appropriately insure yourself.

The first step in determining how much coverage you need is to identify the specific reason you want the coverage. Are you simply covering a debt or obligation, or are you wanting to replace an income to support loved ones?

In the previous chapter, we discussed how to calculate the amount of insurance you need. As you probably recall, we discussed the details for creating income from a death benefit as well as calculating a benefit amount suitable for covering your liabilities and other considerations.

Now, the second step is to determine what type of coverage you should have by first understanding how long you need or want the coverage to last. Do you only need coverage for a few years, or do you need it long term? Typically the responsibility of having children leads to requiring coverage for a specified period of time, such as from the time a child is born up to the time she graduates from college. A more long-term example of life insurance coverage is when you have a pension that will stop if you die, which would leave a spouse in need of additional income sources. In these examples, life insurance acts as the replacement source of income if you were to die.

The third step is to determine how much you want to spend on the coverage and recognizing whether or not you have surplus assets that you want to save into the short term or intermediate categories of your financial plan. (These categories were explained in previous chapters.) This is important because the inherent design of a life insurance policy allows for cash accumulation options, which can be used for specific purposes and helps to narrow down the type of life insurance policy to use. We will discuss this more in a moment.

Two strategic applications of life insurance are:

1. The unique tax rules that surround a life insurance policy. Life insurance uses the FIFO accounting method. FIFO stands for "First In, First Out," which means that the first money to go into the contract—your money—is the first money to be taken out when money is withdrawn. This allows investors to have tax-favored access to their money. Once the cost basis (the amount of money they contributed) is exhausted, a loan provision is available, which allows for the money to be taken out in the form of a loan. By taking the money out in the form of a loan, the policy owner avoids having to pay taxes on the earnings. (Although the loan helps to avoid taxes today, if the contract is canceled, all taxes are ultimately due. If the contract is kept until death, the death benefit is reduced by the amount of the outstanding loan.)
2. A non-recognition loan provision of certain type of life insurance contracts allows the policy owner to access cash without actually removing their money from the policy. Instead, the insurance company lends the policy owner money using the life policy as collateral. (We will discuss this in depth in chapter nine.)

Before we go any further, it would be helpful for you to have a general understanding of the basic types of life insurance and how they can fit into your overall financial plan. Here are outlines of the different types of life insurance, along with the good, bad, and ugly for each type.

Term Life Insurance

Term insurance is the most common and least expensive form of insurance in terms of pricing. For a few dollars a month, you can have hundreds of thousands of dollars in life insurance. People often use this form of insurance when they want to cover the need for life insurance for a specific term (hence the name). These programs can be for a single year or can range up to thirty years before they expire.

The expiration is the drawback to this type of coverage. Although the premiums are lower than any other form of life insurance, the coverage is for a set period, and once the period is over the coverage stops. That means that all the premiums paid along with the coverage are gone. There is no value to the contract unless you die within the term.

Whole Life, or Permanent Life Insurance

The most traditional form of life insurance is a whole life or permanent policy. This policy carries the highest premium of all policy types, requiring a larger cash outlay to own. The difference between a whole life policy and a term policy is that a whole life policy often does not have an expiration date. The contract is guaranteed to be in place until you die, as long as you make the fixed level premium.

In addition, the policy, in its traditional participation structure, offers dividend payments along with a guaranteed cash value, while a term contract has no value other than its death benefit. The cash accumulation characteristics of the contract helps the policy owner offset the higher premiums and over time can achieve earnings ranging from three to five percent. If held long enough, the policy's cash value may exceed the premiums paid, making the policy an efficient form of long-term insurance.

In chapter nine, we dedicate an entire chapter to explaining a strategic use of whole life insurance in your financial planning.

Universal Life Insurance

A hybrid type of policy is known as a universal life policy. This type of policy was created to substitute the use of a traditional whole life policy at a time when interest rates were high which drove the industry to create a program that could benefit from rising interest rates. Unlike a whole life policy, which accumulates cash through guarantees and dividends, universal life is driven by interest rates.

How this works is that the insurance company declares an interest rate for the policy for a specified period (typically a year) then adjusts the rate year to year, depending on the interest rate environment at the time. The policies will normally carry a minimum rate, which can vary but is usually around two or three percent. The premiums for this type of policy are often slightly less than a whole life policy, but can be more than a term contract. These policies are similar to whole life policies, since they provide life insurance coverage until you die (provided the varying premiums are paid).

The main drawback to this type of policy is the unpredictable interest rate environment, along with the internal increase in life insurance cost each year. While a whole life policy's premiums are internally fixed, a universal life policy has a flexible premium, which can be adjusted to accommodate a lower payment into the policy. This can be good, but it can also be a bad thing. Let me explain.

The way this policy works is that the insurance company sets the cost of insurance based on mortality tables. For example it may be fifty dollars per month. Therefore, all you are required to pay to sustain the policy is the fifty dollars per month. However, in the next year, the cost may go up to sixty dollars per month, requiring you to pay a higher premium the next year. This happens each year you own the contract, and over time, the premiums can become unaffordable for most people.

So to prevent this escalation of monthly premiums, the contract is typically arranged to prevent you from having to continually increase the amount you are required to pay each year. This is accomplished by estimating the average cost over the life of the contract. For instance, it may be estimated that $150 per month is an average of the premiums you would pay over a period of time. If you were to make this payment, the extra hundred dollars per month difference in the first year would go into the general account and would earn the interest rate declared by the insurance company. The idea is that the interest earned, along with the premium payments made will satisfy the increase in the internal insurance cost over time.

Variable Universal Life Insurance

Universal life was a popular product at a time when interest rates were high, but as interest rates declined, the policy's appeal diminished, leading insurance companies to design a program with more appeal. That is when a variable component was added to the program, which removed the insurance company's obligation to commit to a set rate and tied the earnings of the contract to the stock market.

A variable universal life policy helps people satisfy the need for life insurance without sacrificing the need and desire to invest. This policy allows people to do both, which is very appealing to a lot of investors.

The drawback to this contract is the fees. All life insurance comes with a cost for the insurance coverage, but with a variable life policy, there are added fees associated with it that can be a drag on the policy, if used for investment purposes. I will not get into all these fees in this book, but understand that this type of contract is reserved for people who have money to invest, and who may not qualify for other traditional tax-favored investments such as Roth IRAs.

A word of caution about this type of contract—since there is an investment component to the policy, a drop in value due to market fluctuation can jeopardize the death benefit if the cash value diminishes, and the internal cost of insurance cannot be covered. (Although many contracts come with a guarantee for the insurance benefit, this guarantee typically does not last the entire life of the contract.)

I do want to clarify my position on all of these types of life insurance policies. There are many circumstances when one type of policy would be used over another. I am not promoting one over the other, nor am I criticizing one over another. As with every recommendation I make, the determining factor is understanding how the decision fits into your personal purpose for the money and identifying how that decision will propel you toward fulfilling your goals.

Guarantees are based on the claims-paying ability of the Issuer and do not protect against market fluctuation. The guarantee only applies to the death benefit and does not cover the sub-account investments. Investing involves risk including the potential loss of principal. No investment strategy can guarantee a profit or protect against loss in periods of declining values.

CHAPTER SEVEN

Investments

The idea of taking hard-earned money and placing it into an investment, which you do not fully understand or realize the risk associated with can be a cause for uneasiness. Many people who bring their investments to me for review often do not know what they have, cannot read their statement, and typically have no contact with the company or advisor that sold the investment to them. It is something they have, but they do not know what to do with it.

Well, it is time for you to take control of your investments! In this chapter, I will help you differentiate one investment from another and will help you to understand the difference between a tax code and a product. Let's get started by breaking down your options, and defining what you may be looking at in your own portfolio.

When you hear terms like *stock* or *equity market*, they are referring to the exchange of stock shares from one person or institution to another. You may hear terms like S&P 500, DOW, NASDAQ, Russell 2000, and others, all of which are created to track different segments of the stock market. They are indexes or barometers for measuring its performance.

Investing involves risk including the potential loss of principal. No investment strategy can guarantee a profit or protect against loss in periods of declining values. Indices are an unmanaged group of securities considered to be representative of the stock market in general. You cannot invest directly in an index. Past performance does not guarantee future results.

A <u>stock</u> is a representation of ownership in a company. Companies issue stock to raise money for their operations. They give away a portion of ownership in exchange for capital. This is where the term equity comes from; if you purchase a share of stock you have equity in the company. *Investment in stocks will fluctuate with changes in market conditions.*

A <u>bond</u> on the other hand is exactly the opposite. It is a debt that a company issues to raise money for their operations. You do not have any ownership in the company but by purchasing a bond you essentially have an IOU with interest from the company. In other words, they are borrowing money from you. The bond market is similar to the stock market in that bonds are traded in an open exchange.

A <u>mutual fund</u> is made up of a number of stocks and bonds, for the purpose of diversification and simplicity. For a fee, a fund manager buys and sells stocks and bonds on your behalf and operates within the boundaries of a given objective. For instance, if you want to invest in China, you can purchase a mutual fund that only buys stocks and bonds in that country. The idea behind a mutual fund is that you have the ability to invest, while having a portfolio manager make the buying and selling decisions. In addition, you have the ability to hold multiple stocks and bonds with a single investment. A mutual fund is not traded on any exchange and is purchased directly through an issuing company. A transaction to purchase or sell a mutual fund is settled at the end of each trading day. The return and principal value of mutual fund shares fluctuate with changes in market conditions. When redeemed, shares may be worth more or less than their original cost. Investments seeking to achieve higher rates of return generally involve a higher degree of risk of principal. Investments in aggressive growth funds tend to be more volatile than the market in general. *Mutual funds are sold by prospectus. Investors should read the prospectus carefully and consider the investment objectives, risks, charges, and expenses of each fund carefully before investing. The prospectus contains this and other information about the investment company. Pleases contact your representative or the investment company to obtain the prospectuses.*

An ETF or Exchange Traded Fund is similar to a mutual fund in its makeup and philosophy but it is traded like a stock on an exchange. The advantage of an ETF over a mutual fund is that it is traded in real time rather than settling at the end of a day. *This type of investment is not suitable for all investors. ETFs will fluctuate with changes in market conditions. In many cases ETFs have lower expense ratios than comparable index funds. However, since ETFs trade like stocks, they are subject to brokerage fees and trading spreads. Therefore, ETFs are not effective for dollar cost averaging small amounts over time, and likewise any strategy using ETFs must account for these additional costs. ETFs do not necessarily trade at the net asset values of their underlying holdings, meaning an ETF could potentially trade above or below the value of the underlying portfolio.*

A REIT or Real Estate Investment Trust takes everything that we know about a mutual fund but is specific to real estate. The difference is that a mutual fund can be purchased or sold at any time where a REIT is only available when there is an offering available to purchase and only allows you to receive your money back when the portfolio making up the REIT as a whole is sold. You may have the ability to retrieve your money before an actual sale for a fee.

A BDC or Business Development Company is structured similar to a REIT except for the underlining investments are different. In a BDC, the underlining investments are primarily tied to various forms of debt.

An annuity is a financial product issued by an insurance company. It allows for tax-deferred growth of money and can provide income at retirement, in specified amounts, for a specified period of time. They are long-term contracts with many benefits, but they do have their limitations, which we will cover here.

There are three basic types of annuities: fixed, indexed, and variable. Let's go through these one at a time.

- A *fixed annuity* is a contract that provides a set interest rate for a specific term. For example, you may have a contract that has a 3% rate for five years. Once the five years is complete, the rate can adjust up or down based on the rate the company declares for the next year. Often, the contract will have a guaranteed minimum rate, which means that after the initial contract term, your rate will not go below a certain rate.

■ *An indexed annuity* is a contract that provides a fixed rate option, which guarantees a rate typically for a one-year period, while also providing an option for an indexed rate. The indexed rate is calculated using a proprietary method, which may include a common index such as the S&P 500 Composite Index. The indexed rate is often limited on its upside potential, while limiting the downside risk. For example, you may have a contract that has a six percent annual cap (which allows a return of up to six percent), and a zero percent minimum (which limits your risk to zero). In an indexed annuity, you are not directly invested into an index.

■ A variable annuity is a long-term investment vehicle designed for retirement purposes. It provides investment options called subaccounts. These subaccounts determine the gain on or loss of your investment, depending on the performance of the chosen investment. There are no guarantees against loss, and no promise of future returns. You have the upside potential of the markets, with the downside risk associated with owning an investment.

Fees can vary fairly significantly depending on the type of contract you own. The following are common contract arrangements and fee structures.

■ A fixed annuity contract could have ongoing fees and a possible annual contract fee. The insurance company builds their profit margin into the rate they offer you. This is similar to how a bank makes money.

■ An indexed annuity is a complex contract with many moving parts. However, it is similar to a fixed-rate annuity in that there could be ongoing fees for the base contract, as well as the profit the insurance company builds into the structure of their crediting method. Early withdrawals from an indexed annuity generally incurs penalties, which may result in a loss in principle invested.

■ A variable annuity has common fees that many insurance companies charge for their base contract. There are mortality and expense charges, along with an administrative charge. These fees are generally a percentage of assets in the contract, often ranging from 1.25% to 4%. In addition, some contracts add a fixed annual contract fee, typically around thirty-five to fifty dollars. *Guarantees are based on the claims-paying ability of the Issuer and do not protect against market fluctuation. The guarantee only applies to the death benefit and does not cover the sub-account investments.*

An annuity will typically carry provisions for how long the owner must hold the contract. This period of time is referred to as the surrender period. This can range from no required surrender period to a period of ten years or more. During this period, there is limited access to the funds in the contract without a penalty. These penalties and withdrawal restrictions are based on each separate investment made in the annuity. One of the most common arrangements is having access to 10% of the initial deposit each contract year. For example, if you deposit $100,000, you may have access to as much as $10,000 per year.

Furthermore, withdrawals from annuities prior to age fifty-nine and a half will incur a ten percent penalty in addition to the payment of any income taxes due.

Annuities offer riders that can be added to an annuity contract to enhance certain features. To clarify, riders are optional. They come at an additional cost and are often subject to specific restrictions and limitations. A few of the most common riders are:

- A *nursing home waiver* is a common rider added to many contracts. This rider could allow for account access if the annuity owner is confined to a nursing home and requires access to the funds in the contract even if within a surrender period.
- A *long-term care rider* is a feature some contracts offer that allows for an enhanced payout benefit based on the amount of assets in the contract, if the annuity owner is in need of long-term care. There is generally an additional fee added to the contract if this rider is elected.
- An *income benefit rider* is a feature some contracts offer that allows a contract owner to receive income from the contract for a specified period of time without initially annuitizing the contract. There is generally an additional fee added to the contract if this rider is elected. (Annuitizing

is an arrangement between an insurance company and the annuity owner, where you essentially hand your principal over to the company in exchange for a guaranteed income for a specified term, which can range from a few years to the lifetime of the owner or surviving spouse.)

This is not an exhaustive list of what annuities are but it is a good start to understanding common arrangements offered by insurance companies.

A CD or Certificate of Deposit is offered through a bank or credit union. It is an arrangement that provides a set interest rate for a specific term. For example, you may have a CD that has a three-percent rate for five years. Once the five years are complete, the bank or credit union will notify you what the declared rate will be for a new term and provide a short window for you to either pull your money out or allow it to renew. A CD is FDIC insured and has guarantees for your principal.

There are many other products available and while there are other viable options, an attempt to cover them all would be a book in and of its self. Rest assured that we have covered the most popular products. I will now move on to explain tax codes.

What I have found to be true is that many people have trouble differentiating between a product and a tax code. They believe that an IRA is what your money is physically in. This is not exactly how this works. A product such as the ones we described earlier in this chapter is what physically holds your money. Once the money is in the product, it is necessary to inform the IRS how we plan to handle our tax liabilities. This is where the tax codes come into play.

- An IRA (Individual Retirement Account) allows you to contribute to the product and take a deduction on your tax return up to certain limits. Money grows tax-deferred, and when you withdrawal money from such an account, a hundred percent of the distribution is subject to tax.

- There are a few different varieties for employer-sponsored retirement plans. For-profit companies typically use a 401k; nonprofits use a 403b; and government entities use a 457 to allow their employees to save through payroll deduction. Although the limits for how much can be contributed to these plans are higher than the limits on an IRA, all accounts have a similar tax treatment.

- A Roth IRA is different than a traditional IRA since the contributions are not tax deductible, growth is tax-free, and withdrawals are tax-free.

This is not an exhaustive list of codes, but it does cover the most common and can help you to understand the difference between a product and a tax code.

CHAPTER EIGHT

Silent Killer

One of the main enemies of saving money is inflation. It is known as the silent killer, and it earns its reputation by its power to slowly deteriorate the purchasing power of our money over time. Inflation impacts our life in small doses, which makes it easy to overlook from one year to the next, but its effects can be problematic in the longer term. Inflation pushes the price of goods and services up, which in turn reduces the standard of living to which people are accustomed, requiring that people earn more money simply to maintain the same lifestyle.

Protecting your investments and saving accounts from inflation is fairly straightforward and involves following some simple math. If you earn two percent on a bank CD, and inflation is running at two percent, you essentially break even. You would not have earned or lost any money. However, there are taxes due on the two percent interest you earned, which results in a net loss. So it is not enough to simply keep up with inflation. You must earn more than the anticipated rate of inflation and taxes combined.

As you can see, determining your break-even point is an easy calculation, but I have to believe that for most people, the idea of just breaking even is not what they dream of when visualizing their financial future. I would contend that many people seek to have their money grow over time in an effort to create wealth for their retirement.

When it comes to planning for retirement, inflation can leave you with a false sense of understanding about how much money you will need in retirement. An inflation rate of two percent seems like a small figure and can even be perceived as an irrelevant amount, but when you multiply this figure over ten years, it translates to twenty percent, or twenty cents on a dollar. In other words, a $50,000 salary today will require you to earn $59,754 in ten years if there is a compounding inflation rate of two percent.

If you make $50,000 today, and plan to retire in twenty years, you will need to have $72,840 of income to live the same lifestyle. It is then important to understand that twenty years into your retirement you will need an annual income of $108,237 to live the same lifestyle that your $50,000 is providing today. So, when you are thinking about how much money you need to save for retirement, remember that you are saving to replace your future income, not your current income.

Years	Future Income	Years	Future Income
1	$50,000.00	21	$74,297.37
2	$51,000.00	22	$75,783.32
3	$52,020.00	23	$77,298.98
4	$53,060.40	24	$78,844.96
5	$54,121.61	25	$80,421.86
6	$55,204.04	26	$82,030.30
7	$56,308.12	27	$83,670.91
8	$57,434.28	28	$85,344.32
9	$58,582.97	29	$87,051.21
10	$59,754.63	30	$88,792.23

11	$60,949.72	31	$90,568.08
12	$62,168.72	32	$92,379.44
13	$63,412.09	33	$94,227.03
14	$64,680.33	34	$96,111.57
15	$65,973.94	35	$98,033.80
16	$67,293.42	36	$99,994.48
17	$68,639.29	37	$101,994.37
18	$70,012.07	38	$104,034.25
19	$71,412.31	39	$106,114.94
20	$72,840.56	40	$108,237.24

Inflation is often a difficult concept to wrap your mind around. The effects of it are obvious but understanding how it is created is a confusing topic for most people. In the remainder of this chapter, we will learn how inflation begins, and why it happens. This will help you to form a basic understanding of pricing of goods and services, our government, the Federal Reserve, and business operations. It can help clarify many misunderstandings for how our economy works and provide you with an appreciation for how intertwined the system really is.

Supply and Demand

If you have ever experienced the desire or the need for something that was in short supply, you likely recall the fact that the item was difficult to find. Other people wanted and were buying the same thing you wanted, limiting the availability of the item. Often when you have an item that is in high demand and there is a limited supply of the item, retailers and manufacturers will increase the price of the item to capitalize on the situation.

However, there is often a balance of supply and demand that stabilizes prices. A company is not going to intentionally produce more of a product than what they believe they can sell, and if the demand is high, they will produce more to satisfy the demand.

An example of how this works is with the world's oil supply. Oil is something that is in high demand, since most of us need it to fuel our vehicles. When we fill up our gas tanks, this triggers a need for more oil to be produced for the next person to fill up. The amount of oil pumped out of the ground to manufacture gasoline is regulated based on how much gasoline is being used. The oil is extracted from the ground and distributed into the market at a sufficiently high level to satisfy the need, but at a sufficiently low level to keep prices stable. Because there is such a high demand for fuel, a sudden shortage of fuel would surely cause the price of a gallon of gas to soar.

Parenthetically, oil is highly political, and it plays a significant role in world economics. Since oil is traded globally using American dollars, the exchange rate of our currency with that of an oil producing country is a contributing factor to the price of a gallon of gas. As the dollar declines and the exchange rate widens, the price of gas goes up. This is an origination point of inflation, leading to people having less money to spend on other things, which in turn has a negative impact on the economy.

Now, imagine for a moment that you have a small business that requires the transport of widgets from one location to another. If there is an increase in the price of a gallon of gas, your fuel costs rise, causing an increase in your transportation costs. To avoid losing money, you are forced to combat this increase by reducing your expenses and increasing revenue. This is accomplished by cutting jobs, closing facilities and increasing the price of your widgets.

The effect of this is an increase in the cost for consumers to purchase the widget, which in turn forces people to reduce other household expenses. Now, people are spending less money on goods and services, which leads to companies not selling enough, which forces the companies to cut more jobs and raise their prices. The effect is a never-ending spiral of job losses and price increases. When this begins to happen, you often see government intervention.

Government

A book by L. Carlos Lara and Robert P. Murphy, *How Privatized Banking Really Works*, does a great job explaining the US banking system. In the book, the authors use the example of the former Roman Empire to explain the impact that inflation and the devaluation of currency has on an economy. The book illustrates the destructive patterns of government, and the influence those patterns have on our daily lives.

In the book, the authors point out that Caesar was a man known for overindulgence and power. The key to his success was his military, which he used to conquer neighboring territories to strip them of their assets, as well as to enforce collecting taxes from the people. This acquired wealth, along with the taxes collected, paid for the expansion and the funding of his military, architecture, and infrastructure.

Over time, Caesar found himself in a situation where he was not collecting enough gold from the people of Rome to pay the expenses he had to keep his empire running. So he had a choice to make: cut spending, or reduce the size of his government. Well, he did not want to do either, so he decided that he would keep doing what he was doing, and he would pay for his expenses by creating more money.

Caesar shaved his gold coins, using the gold collected to make additional coins, which he then used to pay for goods and services. He manipulated the currency being used for commerce within his kingdom and attempted to pass off these (what were essentially) counterfeit coins as the same as before. The result was an increase in his wealth, which enabled him to continue to operate without cutting expenses. However, this backfired on him when the merchants were handed the new coins for goods and services, and noticed that the coins were smaller. The merchants' response to the lighter coins was that they demanded two coins for the same goods and services.

As time went on, Caesar was faced with yet another deficit-spending year, and he responded in the same manner. He attempted to counterfeit the coins again, but the merchants responded by adding safety features to the coins, to allow them to more easily detect if the coins were altered. Now that he was unable to reduce the size of the coins, Caesar decided to melt all the coins down, and then reproduce them using a combination of gold and another metal, which would allow him to make more coins with the same amount of gold. Caesar continued this process until the coins ultimately contained less than one percent gold, rendering the money worthless. Well, we all know what happened to Rome, and unfortunately our modern-day government is repeating the errors of the Romans by spending at unsustainable levels.

The United States of America once used physical gold and silver as currency, then adopted the use of a paper certificate replacing physical gold, for ease of transporting currency. The certificate guaranteed that there was gold somewhere to support its value. In the meantime, our government incrementally reduced the content of silver in our coins until ultimately, it removed the precious metal all together. Then finally, the government took our currency off the gold standard, which divorced our money from the value of gold. More on this in a moment...

The money we now use is called fiat money, or in other words, money made out of thin air. Fiat currency is a form of currency that governments around the world issue and control, so they can fund their obligations. The way this works is that if the government needs more money, they have the ability to create more. Since the government seems to continually need more and more money, they have more and more created. This process devalues our currency, spurring inflation.

Earlier I discussed how rising gasoline prices can create a ripple effect, ultimately leading to inflation and job losses. These are contributing factors to government involvement, since a reduction of income and spending reduces the amount of taxes a government collects. Now, you would think the government would cut back on its spending, just as you and I would if our income was cut, but that is not exactly how our government operates. You would also think that the easy solution to this would be to raise taxes (which our government does do, directly and indirectly), but they also know that they can only tax the population so much before there is dissention. There is a limit to what a government can force its citizens to pay without creating more problems. This leaves the government holding the proverbial bag, unable to cover its obligations. So, just as Caesar did, the government creates more money by literally making more currency.

So how do they do this? In the simplest possible terms, the government issues an IOU to the Federal Reserve Bank, similarly to how you would borrow money from the bank to buy something. They make a promise to the Federal Reserve to repay the money with interest. The Federal Reserve then lends the money to the government, which then uses the money to pay their bills. This process floods the economy with new money (benefiting the government), which causes the dollars already in circulation to be worth less, as a result of having too much money in circulation, similar to the effects of Caesar's actions in ancient Rome.

The key take-away from this is that the Federal Reserve creates money out of thin air to pass on to the government. This is what we have heard about in recent years as "Stimulus" or "Quantitative Easing."

Remember what happened when Caesar flooded the market with manipulated coins? The merchants in turn demanded more coins for the same goods and services. This is what happens in modern times as well, but we have to think on a global scale.

Goods and services, including oil, are traded around the world. The exchange rate between one currency and another is in part how inflation can seep into the system. If we are buying oil from Saudi Arabia, the riyal to dollar exchange rate may be low, forcing the Saudi government to charge more for the oil. This is the same for gold and silver as well. As the dollar goes down in value, the value of gold and silver (along with other precious metals) tends to rise. It is all about conversion rates, supply and demand, and government actions.

Although simplified (but still complicated), these are a few of the mechanisms through which inflation is created. The challenge of inflation is not something to focus, on since you have limited control over how it is created. However, awareness of the fact that it exists is important, since it enables you to combat the erosion of your money's purchasing power. This means saving more money to get to retirement and to sustain your lifestyle throughout retirement.

Combating inflation may seem like an overwhelming task, but the information and strategies provided for you in this book can help position you for success.

Excerpts from How Privatized Banking Really Works used with permission from L. Carlos Lara and Robert P. Murphy

— CHAPTER NINE —

Privatized Banking

In previous chapters we discussed budgeting and managing your expenses to maximize your income. In this chapter we will dig deeper into how money flows in and out of your life. We will be discussing how those educated in the area of privatized banking or infinite banking concepts using a dividend paying whole life insurance contract are attempting to capitalize on this flow of money.

It is staggering to think about the amount of money we earn over a lifetime. If you earn $50,000 per year, over 20 years you will have earned $1,000,000! That's a lot of money and when you calculate the amount of money that will be spent, well that is likely a lot of money too.

Capturing and maintaining control over some of this money while it flows through your hands is the purpose behind this chapter. We will take a look at a strategic concept originated by author Nelson Nash who has been shouting the benefits of using a specially designed dividend paying whole life insurance contract (SDLI) as a private bank for years.

The terminology of "Private Bank" or "Privatized Banking" does not suggest that a policy is an actual bank. The name represents a process of saving or borrowing money that most people associate as activities with a bank. So, the terms "Private Bank" or "Privatized Banking" is referring to the banking activity.

Many of us use banks on a daily basis to make transactions for personal or business purposes. You have income flow into your accounts and you have bills you pay from those accounts. It is a continuous process of earning, spending and replenishing your supply of money to meet the ongoing need you have for it. It's like filling up a gas tank and driving. You have to keep filling the tank in order to have the ability to keep driving.

Aside from these reoccurring obligations, you may have other things you are saving for such as a new car, home improvements, or a child's education among other things. These would be considered big-ticket items that you would save for over time then spend the money in large chunks. You may even find yourself needing to borrow money from a bank to fund these types of transactions.

Regardless of how you approach these big-ticket items, one thing is for certain, you will save and accumulate money then spend it or you will borrow the money then pay the loan off over time. Either way, it is a zero sum game considering all arrows lead to zero and requires a continuous need to earn, spend and replenish your supply of money to be able to make those less frequent but large transactions when they are needed.

To illustrate this point, let's assume you are saving $500 per month to have access to cash every 5 years to purchase a $30,000 automobile using traditional banking methods. When the time comes to purchase the automobile, you write a $30,000 check taking you back to zero while you continue to save $500 per month. The money is now gone forever from your control as you drive off in your car and begin saving for the next purchase in five years. (The same can be said for other big-ticket items in your life such as college, home improvements or vacations.)

So the question becomes, how do you take money that you are already saving and spending and have that money work for you long after you would have otherwise used it. This may sound like a far-fetched idea but using a Specially Designed Life Insurance Contract (SDLI) that is designed correctly can create long-term wealth resulting from money you would have otherwise spent.

To begin to put this concept into perspective, you first need to take everything you have heard about whole life insurance and set it aside. You can hang on to your beliefs about it but understand we are talking about an entirely different use for it. We are going to be talking about a specially designed life insurance contract (SDLI) engineered for utilizing cash. This is very different from the basic approach to buying life insurance.

Now, there are a few key things you should understand about the term "Specially Designed". This concept will not work well unless the contract being used has certain characteristics and the financial advisor who is developing the design for you understands how to use them.

So, a word of caution, if you choose to establish this type of program, make sure you are working with a financial advisor who has a thorough understanding of how this concept works. In addition, make sure the contract being offered is with a mutual insurance company that allows for Paid Up Additions and Non Recognition Loans.

Now, I realize that you may have little understanding of what all of this means so let me explain:

- A mutual life insurance company simply means that the company is a private company and is not stockowner owned. If a company is a mutual company then its policy owners technically own it. This benefits you since the boards of directors are not accountable to share holders but rather the policyholders.
- A non-recognition loan is a loan provision where the insurance company will loan you money from their assets using your death benefit (if you pass away) and cash surrender value (while you are alive) as collateral up to the amount of cash surrender value you have in the policy. This allows for your entire cash value to remain inside the contract and continue earning dividends and interest.
- LPUA or a Level Paid Up Addition rider allows policy owners to add more money to the policy than just the required premium of the contract. This provision provides an advantage to the policy owner since they can rapidly accumulate cash to build their "banking system" while also purchasing addition insurance that is paid up.

Now, when the term "whole life insurance" comes up in a conversation, many people will begin to dismiss this form of insurance stating that it is too expensive and the rate of return is too low compared to other programs. In some ways they are correct. If you simply want to purchase life insurance then this is probably not the best type of program to use. In previous chapters we discussed term insurance as an affordable way to carry life insurance coverage. If you want to invest long term, there are potentially better programs available that offer direct or indirect exposure to markets.

So, yes, in some ways what they are saying is correct. However, we are not talking about investing long term with this concept nor are we talking about simply buying life insurance. The idea is for this to be used as a cash alternative or bank alternative not an investment alternative or a basic life insurance solution. We are talking about fulfilling the need for capital on an ongoing basis using the cash value of the insurance policy.

Now, how does a whole life insurance policy allow access to cash and how does this benefit the policy owner?

As we already discussed, a SDLI contract has a specific feature designed to allow the policy owner access to money through a non-recognition loan from the insurance company. In other words, the insurance company will loan you money from their assets using your death benefit and cash surrender value as collateral up to the amount of cash surrender value you have in the policy. This allows for your entire cash value to remain inside the contract and continue earning dividends and interest as if you did not take any money from the policy. It is uninterrupted compounding growth!

This is an important point to grasp because without fully understanding this loan provision it will be difficult to understand why anyone would use this concept in their financial planning.

Let me give an example, you have $10,000 in a bank account earning interest and you withdrawal $4,000 from the account, the amount of money remaining and earning interest is $6,000.

Common sense, right?

Now lets look at the general concept behind a SDLI contract and assume you have the same $10,000 in the policy earning dividends and you withdraw $4,000 in the form of a loan. Using a SDLI contract, the amount of money remaining and earning dividends is $10,000. The contract functions as if the money was never removed from the policy because technically it never was removed. The insurance company lends the $4,000 to you from their assets and only uses your policy as collateral.

You may ask why the insurance company would do this. From their position, it is a simple and safe investment to lend money to their policy owners at a competitive interest rate. If you think about it, they have millions of dollars coming in each month from other policy owners who are paying their premiums and they need to invest the money somewhere. By lending the money to their own policy owners and charging interest, they have the collateral of their own policy to back the loan. They feel it is a pretty safe bet.

On the topic of interest charged on the loan, there is a cost to doing business and in order for the insurance company to offer this method of accessing money from your policy there needs to be a benefit for them to make the loan. However, through a properly designed SDLI contract, you may be able to recapture the interest paid on the loan through the dividends earned in the policy.

Let me explain.

The benefit of using a SDLI contract is that it provides an opportunity for you to have your money remain in the policy and continue to grow while simultaneously using a policy loan from the insurance company to access money.

For example, you have $100,000 in cash value within your SDLI contract earning 4% and you take a loan of $30,000 to purchase an automobile at 5% from the insurance company. By taking the money as a loan, your $100,000 remains in the policy and continues to grow uninterrupted. Therefore, in our example, the $100,000 earns $4,000 and the loan interest on the $30,000 loan is $1,500. The earnings on your cash value recaptured the loan interest paid. ($4,000 Earned- $1,500 Paid = $2,500 Net)

One thing to keep in perspective is that when it comes to people who are good savers, they tend to have money available when they need it. They save regularly and seldom need every dollar they have at any one time. They have money flow into their life and they have money flow out of their life but are habitual savers. If you are someone who always needs every dollar that you have, then perhaps this is not the best approach for you at this time.

This concept can be most advantageous when used by a business owner who is investing into their business. If they have uninterrupted compound growth within their policy and recapturing the interest paid on their loan while using the money they borrowed to expanded their business and profit from their investment, not only did they have an internal rate of return in their policy but they also have an external rate of return on their investment using the same pool of money!

Now, this brings us to the next layer in this concept - repayment of the loan.

The loan on a SDLI contract has flexibility since the insurance company does not have a required repayment schedule. From the insurance companies perspective, they can charge you interest every year on the loan and know that if you die the loan is repaid or if you surrender the contract they deduct the loan balance plus interest before they send you the proceeds from your contract. Either way, they know the loan will be repaid. So, they are not concerned whether you ever make a payment toward the loan.

However, from a policy owner standpoint, not repaying the loan limits access to money in the future but for some situations this still can be an advantage over paying cash considering the recapturing example we used a moment ago.

There are other personally tailored ways to work a loan. If the company allows you to pay your principal first then you can simply pay the principal of a loan and leave the interest to accumulate or perhaps you pay the interest and leave the principal. There is a lot of flexibility making the concept of SDLI a viable strategy for a variety of situations.

Clearly in a privatized banking arrangement, it is to your advantage to repay the loan since you are likely to want to use money again in the future and by repaying the loan it will allow for more access to money later. Remember, this is all about how cash flows in and out of your life. This design is a conduit to creating more available money than by simply paying cash or financing purchases through a bank.

One other very unique benefit to using a life insurance policy to consider is its tax-favored treatment. The earnings within the policy are tax-free. The money grows tax-free, the death benefit is tax-free and loans are tax-free.

Now, as with every strategy or view I have explained in this book, I want to equip you in making educated decisions for your personal financial situation. The use of SDLI has its limitations and there are things you should consider before implementing this strategy.

The biggest determining factor in whether or not you should consider the use of this strategy is to be honest with yourself and determine if you are a "good" saver. If you have poor money habits and do not have a solid track record of saving money then this strategy is not a good fit.

The reason is due to the temporary illiquidity of cash within the contract. Any person setting up a SDLI strategy needs to understand that they will not have access to 100% of their money for up to 5 to 7 years, depending on the age and health of the insured and the capitalization or funding by the owner. The lack of liquidity covers the cost of the permanent life insurance and to disregard the lack of liquidity would be careless.

The entire foundation of this strategy is built on having access to money (not necessarily all of your money). Therefore, utilizing the available cash value while you wait for all of your money to be accessible is a strategic way to minimize the impact of the temporary illiquidity. But again, if you are someone who needs access to all of your money immediately (from day one), this strategy may not be a good fit. That is why it is important for someone considering this strategy to work with a seasoned financial professional who looks at your entire financial situation before making any recommendation.

In addition, understanding the tax rules is critical when designing SDLI to help avoid an accidental or purposeful MEC (Modified Endowment Contract). How a contract is funded (capitalized) and how withdrawals or policy loans are taken needs to be done carefully to prevent adverse tax ramifications. Also, if a contract is surrendered or were to lapse while the insured is still alive, there could be negative income tax consequences. Be certain that the financial professional(s) you are working with understand the section of the IRS Tax Code that pertains to permanent life insurance (IRC Section 7702).

Proper capitalization (funding) of SDLI can minimize a lot of potential problems being mentioned. If you do not fund the contracts in a manner where the base of the contract and LPUA rider is maximized within the first 3-5 years, it is possible that the policy could underperform causing your cash value growth to be less than expected. Underperformance would then be magnified as the contract experiences loan activity. If you are planning to utilize the policy early in its setup (within the first 24 months), it is imperative that you continue to capitalize the policy through year five or at least begin a payback of the policy loan in some capacity. The compounding impact of the interest accumulating in a policy that has early loan activity without proper capitalization or loan payback could very well result in a SDLI strategy lapsing or requiring unfavorable modifications.

I know this is a lot of information but as with every idea described in this book, you have to understand when something is appropriate for your situation and when it simply is not a good fit.

— CHAPTER TEN —

Asset Allocation

Most everyone has heard the saying, "Don't put all your eggs into one basket." It is used as a cautionary suggestion to not rely on one thing for the results you are seeking. Over the years it has become a buzzword used by many financial advisors and investors when they suggest building a portfolio of investments. It is translated to imply the importance of spreading your risk among multiple holdings. Placing your proverbial eggs into only one basket can leave you vulnerable, too dependent on the performance of that one basket. By having multiple baskets, you can spread your risk around, which in theory will reduce your risk exposure and help insulate you against the fluctuations of the market.

Although this is good advice to follow, I believe that there is a misunderstanding of what is involved with diversifying a portfolio. This belief derives from my experience of reviewing a good number of portfolios. Often, I see people (financial advisors included) doing exactly the opposite, instead following the words of Mark Twain who said, "Put all your eggs in one basket and watch that basket."

Considering the fact that there are a variety of different mindsets about investing, it is impossible to offer a one-size-fits-all suggestion for how to build your portfolio. The goal of this chapter is to help you create a way of thinking about how to design a portfolio. I will walk you through what I believe is the best approach for diversifying a portfolio and help you understand the logic behind it.

Now, since we have been using baskets as our metaphor, let's run with it a bit longer and assume you have a basket made of bamboo. Now, regardless of whether you have one bamboo basket or ten, you still have only bamboo baskets. So regardless of how many bamboo baskets you acquire, you have to understand that you do not create diversification by having many bamboo baskets. You just end up carrying around a lot of bamboo baskets.

In order to wrap your mind around diversification, we should redefine what a basket represents, and how to mix and match these baskets to create a portfolio. An *asset allocation* is by definition the process of choosing asset classes that will help to diversify your risk into segments of the global market. In other words, an asset class is a group of similar investments that make up a certain region, industry, or sector of the market. In our example, bamboo baskets would be an asset class. Here are a few examples of what I am describing:

- Real estate
- Emerging markets
- United States equities
- High yield bonds
- Corporate bonds
- Private equity
- Commodities
- Futures
- Cash
- International equities
- Global bonds

International investing entails special risk considerations, including currency fluctuations, lower liquidity, economic and political risks, and differences in accounting methods. Past performance cannot guarantee future results.

These are just a few. The connection I am trying to help you make is that having multiple baskets of the same type does not constitute diversification, even though you have more than one basket. In order to have diversification, there must be a variety of different types of baskets.

Over the years, I have had many new clients come into my office with money invested into brokerage accounts that include several holdings. When reviewing the holdings to see what they have and investigating how the portfolio is positioned, what I often find is that while they may have several holdings, it is usually made up of only two or three asset classes, which supports my belief that many people (including financial advisors) do not have a solid grasp on what it takes to create a diversified portfolio. The reason for this is easily diagnosed when you consider these two things:

- People tend to have multiple investments with the impression that they are spreading their money around without fully understanding what they are doing. For instance, you can own three different mutual funds that all have similar holdings. One mutual fund may own XYZ Corporation, while the other two own the same company and so on. So even though you have multiple mutual funds, they can at times be invested in pretty much the same things.

- People are attracted to performance and tend to base their investment decisions on what an investment did over the past few years. When looking through a list of investments, often the first thing people recognize is how well the investment has done over the last one, five, or ten year period. Then investors migrate to the best performing investments. The problem with this approach is that it does not tell you the full story and can mislead you into believing that because something has done well in the past that it will continue to do so in the future. This is simply not true. There are many economic, political, and financial influences in the market that can impact performance, and these events may not be repeated, leaving past performance irrelevant.

To get to the next level with diversification, I would encourage you to break out of this antiquated mindset. You should develop a new way of thinking about investing and create a philosophy focused on growing and protecting money.

As a kid or a parent, you have probably been at a playground and have seen the teeter-totter, or seesaw. It is a long board with a fulcrum in the middle. One child sits on one end of this long board, and another child sits on the opposite side. When one child goes up, the child on the other side goes down. When it comes to asset allocation, asset classes can behave in this same manner. This is called having an inverse relationship, and it is what we strive to capture when we diversify among a variety of different asset classes. This opposite movement helps to overcome the loss realized within one investment by experiencing gains in another.

You may have seen the mattress commercial where you have a glass of wine sitting on the bed on one side and on the other side a women is jumping up and down. Although the woman is jumping up and down, the bouncing motion has no effect on the glass of wine. The commercial illustrates that the mattress can have movement on one side that does not affect the rest of the bed. When designing a portfolio, the non-correlation between asset classes is what we strive for when we diversify amongst a variety of different investments. The idea is that the performance of one asset class should have little if any impact on another asset class, preventing losses from becoming viral. In other words, if one investment experiences a loss, you reduce the likelihood of your entire portfolio suffering a loss.

By combining asset classes that possess inverse relationships, coupled with asset classes that are non-correlating, you position yourself for the best probability for long-term success. If you find yourself invested in only one asset class (regardless of the number of holdings you have), you are susceptible to the movement and market conditions of that one class. This can work in your favor if your timing is right, or it can backfire if your timing is poor.

The truth is that no one knows what direction the market will go in, what investment will perform well, or how certain asset classes will behave. Even a day trader, who has the knowledge of what to watch and when to respond, is unable to know with certainty what to do and when to do it. Investing is merely speculation, which supports the value of diversifying across not only many investments (baskets), but also (and more specifically) many asset classes.

When building a portfolio, you have to define how you will approach your investment decisions. Will your decisions be based on short-term movements and the headlines of the day? Or will you take a long-term, balanced approach? If you are chasing returns and making decisions based on what you are hearing in the news and on the radio, then you should stop reading this book and go pick up a day-trading subscription. However, if you prefer a long-term, balanced approach focused on growing and protecting your money, then you are on the right path to diversification.

– CHAPTER ELEVEN –

Managing Investment Risk

Have you ever been at an amusement park where they have a bridge, with a spinning drum surrounding the bridge? The drum has an optical illusion printed onto it and it is illuminated with a black light. You cannot see the actual bridge you are walking across, because it is pitch black, and the illusion of the spinning drum has you so disoriented that it is difficult to even walk. I have been on such a bridge, and let me tell you, it is a very insecure feeling. To say I inched my way across would be an understatement. I moved slowly along the bridge, gripping the railing firmly as I made my way across to the other side. Even though I knew what was going on, and I could see the end of the tunnel twenty feet away, I was still uncomfortable and anxious to get out of the tunnel.

The stock market can be a similar experience. Like they were navigating a twirling tunnel, many people can be left feeling disoriented and confused about their investments. After all, no one can predict the future of the stock market, and there is no guarantee against loss. Simply put, inherent in the stock market is the risk of losing money! So it is understandable that people have some level of uncertainty about their portfolio. The key to overcoming some of the anxiety associated with investing is managing risks and preventing them from paralyzing your decision-making process.

There is some level of risk associated with nearly everything we do. Driving, for instance, carries risk. You could hit someone with your vehicle, or someone could hit you, causing damage to both vehicles. So what is our process for handling the financial risk of driving?

- We accept the risk that if we are in an auto accident and our car is totaled, we will buy a new car. We understand the odds are high for a safe arrival at our destination without the need to worry about an accident.
- We can manage the risk by driving defensively, with our hands on the steering wheel at ten and two, while keeping one foot on the brake. Staying highly alert while driving, without the radio or cell phone to distract us, perhaps lowers our risk of an accident.
- We can purchase auto insurance and pass the financial risk onto the insurance company. Most drivers cover their risk by purchasing insurance, which transfers the risk away from the driver and onto the insurance company. If we are in an accident, we make a call to our insurance agent, and the rest is on them to get the vehicle back to new.
- We could avoid the risk altogether and not drive. There is public transportation and other options for getting from one place to another, and thus we can avoid risk altogether.

So how do we apply this to investing? The fact is that investing in the stock market can make us money; otherwise we would not do it. However, just as with driving, there is financial risk when investing. We can lose money as a result of a market downturn. We can lose money from government actions. We can lose money from a news headline. There is risk all around the markets. So what is our process for handling the financial risk?

- We can simply accept the risk that if money is lost, we will move on and find another investment. The acceptance of risk goes hand in hand in terms of investing. You put your money into the market with the hope of outpacing inflation, and compounding your earnings for future use. Meanwhile, it is essential to understand that market conditions could diminish your anticipated investment. We can look at history and see that while history does not guarantees future results, it does provide insight into past performance and trends. That gives us the knowledge and understanding of what could happen as a result of making an investment. In other words, we can anticipate growth, but we really do not know what the actual outcome will be.

■ We can manage the risk through asset allocation and diversification. There are investments that make money if an investment goes up, while there are other investments that make money if an investment goes down. At the same time, there are investments that historically perform well when another investment performs poorly. Having a mix of investments that cover many different markets can help to soften the ups and downs.

■ We can insure our risk by passing it onto to an insurance company, just as we would the risk associated with our automobiles. Banks and insurance companies offer programs that allow you to pass the risk of a market loss onto them, for a fee of course.

■ We can avoid the risk altogether and simply not invest. This approach eliminates market risk by avoiding the direct influence of the markets. By sticking with CDs or fixed annuity accounts, we avoid the risk inherit in the market. It is important to note that although we can avoid the market risks, we remain exposed to inflation risk. (Inflation risk is the potential erosion of earning potential over time.)

As you can see, there are different ways to manage risk, and depending on your personality, your investment experience, your belief system about money and your phase of life, you will need to determine for yourself which approach make the most sense for you.

The most crucial step is that you must first identify why you are investing. We have already discussed—and will discuss again in other chapters—the importance of understanding the purpose for your money. I won't be repetitive by explaining it more here, but I do want to reiterate how relevant it is to understand why you are doing what you are doing. If you fall into the trap of making a decision based on what sounds good, you run the risk of being sold a product without a full understanding of how it ties into your ultimate purpose for the investment.

While many people are accustomed to having data and sales literature as the driving force for their decision-making, your life phase (which we defined in an earlier chapter) should be your filter of what is or is not appropriate for you. In addition, your risk tolerance should guide you to reaching a level of comfort for how you manage your risk.

Here are some general guidelines to help you identify the level of risk you can tolerate, and how you may want to approach your decision about what type of investment to use.

- If you are a free spirit and believe that investments are more likely to go up than down, I would suggest a mix of growth investments with various capitalization. This is an aggressive, long-term approach to investing.

- If you are of the mindset that investments are the way to go, but you want to limit volatility across the portfolio, then I would look at a multi-asset class allocation

- If you want to participate in market returns but do not want to risk losing money, I would suggest a market-linked CD, or an equity index annuity.

- If you are saving for retirement and are concerned about the possibility of losing money before you retire, or you fear running out of money once you are retired, an annuity may be a good option, since they offer income guarantees that often will last your lifetime.

- If you are scared of the market or simply do not understand it, stay out of it.

Guarantees are based on the claims-paying ability of the Issuer and do not protect against market fluctuation. The guarantee only applies to the death benefit and does not cover the sub-account investments. Investing involves risk including the potential loss of principal. No investment strategy can guarantee a profit or protect against loss in periods of declining values.

It is important to keep in mind when you are investing that picking an investment is not the same as financial planning. I have said it before, and I believe it is worth saying again—anyone can invest in the market. You can go online or to a neighborhood brokerage company to buy an investment, like you would buy a pair of shoes. It's easy, convenient and can even be cheaper than working with an actual financial advisor. If you have the knowledge and confidence to do it on your own, I say go for it.

However, when it comes to distribution and the actual use of your money, it is not as simple and can actually be problematic if your portfolios and accounts are not arranged properly. That is often why I recommend using a professional, since he can help shine light on things that perhaps you are not thinking about.

The bottom line is that if you have questions about what investments to choose or are unsure of exactly what it means to distribute your money, then I highly recommend seeking out a competent financial advisor who has the experience and the ability to assist you in making smart choices. I have an entire chapter in this book dedicated to helping you find an advisor who is right for you.

— CHAPTER TWELVE —

Retiring With a Plan

Reaching the destination of retirement can be an exciting point in your life, as you begin to do the things you have been waiting a lifetime to do, like spending time with kids and grandkids, traveling and volunteering, or perhaps starting the second half of your life with something new.

Whatever your plans are for retirement, what I have found to be true is that many people worry that the income they have in retirement may not be enough to sustain their lifestyle, and they fear running out of money. There is a fear that the retirement they envision may have to be supplemented with a part-time job or a reduction in lifestyle. Although this certainly may be true for some, this mindset is often associated with a misunderstanding of what a retirement plan is. By definition, a retirement plan will eliminate these fears and provide a realistic view of the longevity of income sources.

Throughout this chapter, we will define what a retirement plan looks like and help you to develop a strategy that will help sustain your lifestyle for the rest of your life. When you boil it down, retirement planning has four components:

- Understanding how to invest for income and creating a mindset for retirement
- Establishing a realistic budget
- Positioning your assets to support your spending and income needs in retirement
- Saving enough while you are working to have the ability to transition from earned income to unearned income

In this chapter, we will touch on all four of these components of a retirement plan and will begin creating a powerful mindset for how you save money. This mindset will help to overcome the complexities of how to take an asset and convert it to produce an income. It will shed light onto how your income, taxes, and spending come together in the end to prevent the confusion that typically accompanies a lack of understanding of what makes up a retirement plan.

Imagine for a moment that you are retired and enjoying the benefits of a lifetime of saving and planning. You are receiving a monthly income that covers your living expenses, travel, and entertainment, while you do the things you have been waiting a long time to do. Your health is good, and you can foresee another twenty or more years of life volunteering and spending time with your family.

Now, imagine getting to retirement age and realizing that you have not done enough to be able to stop working. You discover that you need to work a few more years before you can even consider retirement. You have debts to pay and almost nothing left over to save each month, making retirement unrealistic until you can get your finances in order.

In my experience, you will likely find yourself in one of the two described scenarios, either by default or through careful planning. Whichever scenario you choose, understand that you are making a choice. Taking the time to develop a retirement plan or doing nothing to plan your retirement are both strategies that have an outcome. You will either be forced to mold your lifestyle to the income you have available, or you will have the money you have saved for income purposes support the lifestyle of your choosing.

We discussed in an earlier chapter the importance of having a budget for making the most of the income you earn. As we have already identified, a budget is the nucleus for how you position your assets and is what will ultimately determine when you can retire, and how long your assets will last.

There is a temptation for many people who have operated without a budget, and who have gotten by without paying much attention to their spending, to brush off the importance of this step. If this is you, I caution you against taking this approach for your retirement planning needs. In my experience, unless you have stacks of money that you will never use, you are likely going to need to maximize the majority of the money you have saved or inherited.

A common misconception about retirement is that your expenses will be less after you have retired. The reality is that retirement does not necessarily mean that your income needs will decrease. This may be true if you plan to sit on the couch and not do anything with all this new-found free time but you may be surprised to know that your expenses are likely to stay the same, unless your financial obligations change.

A good exercise to help determine the differences between your income needs while you are working, and your income needs when you are retired, is to create a budget that you think will be a good representation of what your spending will be in retirement. Include such things as health care, home improvements, vehicle replacement, long-term care, traveling expenses, hobbies, and charitable activities that you plan to get involved in.

Keep in mind that you will be retired, which means you will have no overtime or bonuses to get "caught up" on lifestyle expenses. Retirement-planning requires you to develop a mindset of living long-term off of what you have right now. This way of thinking alone is enough to help you understand the magnitude of what is involved with securing a comfortable retirement.

So what does a retirement plan look like, and how does it work? Throughout this entire book we have been discussing mindsets, defining the purpose of your money, budgets, investing, and insurance. We will now take a look at how all of this converges, and why all of these things play a role when it comes time to use your money.

Let's consider hypothetically that you are preparing to retire and have $500,000 in your 401k account, and another $200,000 in an IRA. You have $80,000 sitting in a bank account, and another $50,000 in mutual funds. Your home is valued at $250,000 and is paid off.

Your budget shows that you need $7000 per month to pay your bills. Your Social Security benefits are $2000 per month, and you have another $1500 per month from a pension, leaving a difference of $3500 per month that you need your investments to supplement.

Your 401k and IRA account have never been taxed, making any distribution from the accounts a taxable event. Social Security is not taxed until you have exceeded certain thresholds of income, which begin at $32,000 if you're married, and $25,000 if you're single.

Two things to consider through this plan design are these:

1. A basic rule of thumb for distribution calculations is five percent for income. Although there is no guarantee of this type of return in a low-interest rate environment, a well-managed portfolio, or an annuity with an income benefit, are viable options for creating the income you need.
2. Taxes are an important consideration for you, since all the figures we are using here are gross numbers and are subject to tax liability.

The amount of income you can assume you will receive from your IRA is $10,000. Another $25,000 from your 401k brings your total income from qualified accounts to $35,000 per year, or $2,916 per month. Combine this income with your Social Security and pension income, and you will find that you have come within $84 per month of your income needs.

In addition, there is $80,000 in savings. This is money that by our definitions does not have a purpose. So if we consider that your cash reserves should equate to approximately six months of expenses ($42,000), it would be advisable to keep this amount of money in a savings account and take the difference of $38,000 from this pool of money and transfer it to an intermediate account. Combine this $38,000 from savings with the $50,000 in mutual funds and that leaves you with $88,000 in your intermediate account.

This $88,000 in the intermediate account would be best invested in a well-managed, low- to medium-risk investment portfolio, which will allow you to transfer funds to your short-term account if funds are running low, or allows you to adjust your income strategy if inflation becomes more than earnings on your income sources. It is your utility account, and it needs to remain at least partly liquid.

Although there is no way to create a financial plan designed specifically to satisfy your unique situation by reading this book, this strategy is a good template for beginning your retirement planning, and it is a start to understanding how to match your money with your income needs.

When it comes to investing your income sources (IRA and 401k from our example), it would be helpful for you to look again at the chapter on managing risk, and the chapter on investments. These two chapters tie into what we need to understand in order to properly arrange your money for long-term sustainability.

As you approach retirement, your investment philosophy may have been more growth-oriented, based on the fact that you still have time on your side. If the markets slump, you presumably have time to recover the loss. However, as you enter into retirement, you may not have sufficient time to recover from a possible market downturn. Your financial future now rests on how much money you have at that particular moment. This perspective may cause you to consider changing your thinking rather dramatically toward the preservation of your retirement nest egg as you approach this time in your life. The idea of recovery periods from market losses has evaporated leaving any downward fluctuation in your accounts a cause for your income to necessarily drop.

What I hope you take away from this chapter is the understanding that arranging a retirement strategy goes beyond stock picking and hoping that everything will work out. Retirement is a critical juncture in your life that requires a fair amount of planning and evaluation. So I encourage you to take the time to look at the big picture, create the proper mindset for retirement, and position yourself for the best probability of success.

CHAPTER THIRTEEN

Taxes

In 1862, President Abraham Lincoln imposed the first income tax, to help fund the Civil War. The tax was repealed in 1872, then later reappeared in 1894 but was ruled unconstitutional by the US Supreme Court in 1895. The current tax system was set in place with the passage of the Sixteenth Amendment in 1909 under President Howard Taft and became official in 1913 under President Woodrow Wilson. The tax code began with four hundred pages of explanation and after a hundred years, the number of pages in our tax code has grown to over 73,000.

Ever since the tax rules were put into place, people have been trying to figure out ways around them. What we will cover in this chapter is creating a mindset about taxes that goes beyond filing a tax return and focuses on positioning your money to keep more of it for yourself.

I will not get into tax rates or laws since I am not a tax professional. What we will focus on is creating a filter for how to think through whether or not to take advantage of a proposed tax strategy. This filter is simple and comes in the form of a question. Here it is, "Am I saving taxes or am I deferring taxes?" What this question offers is a way to help you determine the benefit of a particular tax strategy. If you are simply deferring taxes then you are really not accomplishing much of anything. You will either pay taxes now or pay taxes later. On the other hand, if there is a legitimate tax savings, then the strategy may be a viable option to consider.

What I have found over the years is that many people will approach taxes with a short-term perspective, focused only on what their tax bill is for a given year. They fund retirement accounts to their maximum levels and take steps to limit their tax bill for the current year at any cost. The problem with this mindset is that it has a tendency to backfire down the road by creating larger tax ramifications when you begin using the money. We will walk through a few scenarios to help you get a fresh perspective on how to approach the more common tax situations.

First of all, if you are teetering between one tax bracket and another, it may make sense to open a tax-deductible savings account. I say that it *may* make sense, because there are many variables to this that may not make it a good idea, but let's just look at it for what it is for now. If a fifteen-percent tax bracket caps out at $35,000, and your income is $38,000 after all your deductions, you would have $3,000 of your income subject to a twenty-five percent tax rate. However, you can reduce your tax exposure by ten percent on the $3,000 by depositing the money into a tax-deductible account such as an IRA or 401k. This essentially saves you $300 by deferring the money until later, assuming all things are equal when you retire.

The mistake I see people make from a tax-planning perspective is deferring taxes when they are in one of the lowest tax brackets to begin with. For instance, if a person makes $30,000 a year, and contributes to his 401k at work, he is essentially doing two things: First of all, the deposit into the account does not generate a tax savings but simply defers the taxes until a later date. Second, he is deferring taxes he could pay now, while he is in a low tax bracket, to a time when he might be in a higher tax bracket down the road.

Over the years, we have seen our tax system become more and more difficult to understand, as the number of rules expand and the tax brackets change with each administration. This trend makes it nearly impossible for anyone to predict with certainty what tax rates a person will be subject to when she reaches retirement. So when it comes to how we approach long-term tax planning, we must work off of what we know to be true, which is that taxes can do one of three things in the future:

1. They can go up.
2. They can stay the same.
3. They can go down.

Since we have no idea what our lawmakers will do from one year to the next, we are forced to plan for the worst and hope for the best. If we use this philosophy when preparing our financial plans, we can have some protection from negative tax policies.

Let me give you a couple more variables to consider. For those of us with children, there are tax credits and deductions that help reduce our current tax liability. As our children grow up and become self-sufficient, we lose those tax benefits. In addition, there are other tax deductions that may go away in the future, either as a result of our government tinkering with the tax code, or by the nature of the deduction itself. For example, many people enjoy the added tax deduction of mortgage interest each year. However, by design, the interest deduction slowly evaporates as you pay down the loan, which often occurs around retirement time.

The point here is that there are two sizable deductions that you have working for you during your working years that may not be available when you are retired. So adding more deductions through retirement accounts, coupled with the existing deductions that gradually dissolve over time, leaves you deferring tax liabilities until retirement, only to have the money taxed then, with few if any deductions available to offset the liability. In addition, if you are successful with accumulating retirement assets, you could very well be deferring your tax liability to a time when you are in the highest tax bracket of your life.

Social Security is another reason to work now at keeping your taxes low in retirement. When you begin receiving benefits, the portion of your Social Security that is subject to federal tax depends on how much income you have to report. If your taxable income is below $25,000 as a single taxpayer or $32,000 if married, filing jointly, none of your Social Security benefits will be taxed. If your income exceeds this amount, then fifty percent of your benefit becomes taxable until you reach $34,000 of income as a single taxpayer, or $44,000 if married, filing jointly. Once your income exceeds this amount, eighty-five percent of your benefits become taxable.

What makes up your taxable income in retirement? The following are examples of taxable income:

- Investment and savings earnings
- Retirement account distributions from IRA, 401k, 403b and other tax deferred accounts.
- Employment earnings
- Social Security
- Pensions

These are a few, but this is certainly not an exhaustive list. The point is that your retirement income could potentially be more than you think, making the decision to contribute to a tax-deductible account a question of how much tax you want to pay in retirement.

When it comes to retirement planning, how much money you have is not as important as knowing how much money you get to keep. If you have one million dollars in a 401k at your work, all of that money is taxable when you begin to use it. Regardless of what tax rates are when you retire, that money is taxable. Having money in a tax-free account leaves you with control over how much money you draw to fund your budget and helps you keep your tax liabilities to a minimum.

Think of it this way. If you had the foresight to begin properly planning now for how you will be receiving your income at retirement, would you plan to have your income taxable or tax-free? How much different would your tax situation be if you had all your money in a tax-free account, versus money in a 401k? For one, your Social Security would not be subject to taxes since the income from a tax-free account does not count against you on your tax return. In addition, current tax law favors lower-income filers by providing tax credits and effectively gives more money back in the form of a tax refund from the IRS than what you paid in.

A Roth IRA, Roth 401k, municipal bonds, or a reverse mortgage can provide you with tax-free streams of income in retirement and depending on your tax situation, there are other, more complex options such as life insurance or pension rescue strategies that can also lead to favorable tax treatment. I will not get into these here, but I do want to reiterate the point of this chapter, and that is to ask whether you are saving tax, or deferring tax. This question will help you avoid common mistakes when it comes to saving money and can help you make sound financial decisions.

CHAPTER FOURTEEN

Your Home's Equity

After saving for retirement and paying for college, people most often say that their top priority is paying off their home mortgage. This, they think, will give them the ability to begin saving money. At other times, this is also a desire to remove their mortgage from their liabilities in the event of a job loss or other unforeseen circumstance, which might leave them vulnerable to losing their home.

In both instances, having a home paid off is a means to having something else. It is a stepping stone to obtaining security, or the ability to save money that would otherwise be used to pay the mortgage payment. Either way, it is important to stop and think about how your approach will affect your overall financial plan.

When it comes to a house and its mortgage, I believe that people often miss the big picture and get so caught up in the short-term mindset of paying off the mortgage that they overlook the ancillary opportunities that come along with owning a house. When you stop and think about it, your home is unlike anything else in your life. It is used on a daily basis; yet it appreciates over time. What else does this? Everything you purchase for consumption is used up or depreciates over time.

To begin to understand the uniqueness of your home, imagine for a moment two identical homes, side by side on a street. The homes have exactly the same features, square footage, landscaping, and color. The only thing that separates them from one another is their address. Now, let's assume that both homes are valued at $100,000 and over the next year they appreciate by 5%. Let's add another variable to this scenario: one of the homes is fully mortgaged, while the other is completely paid off. Now, knowing what you know, what is the respective value of these two houses? Is one worth more, since one has a mortgage? Is the one that is completely paid off worth more than the other?

The fact is that the mortgage does not change the value of the property. In other words, the house does not know that it has a mortgage, and that does not affect the overall value. Therefore, both homes (the one with a mortgage, and the one without) are valued at $105,000. If you sold the house and cashed out the equity, then your net profits would be the selling price, minus any mortgage balance. Yet the home itself would be sold for the same amount, whether or not it had a mortgage. This reality is important to understand as we move on to discuss the use of your home as a financial asset.

Now, if your home has the same value, whether or not it has a mortgage, what would you assume the equity in your home is earning in terms of rate of return? The answer is that the equity in your home is actually earning zero, because the house itself is appreciating, not the equity. The equity increases not by earnings, but by the house's appreciation and mortgage reduction.

In terms of paying off the actual mortgage, let's assume that you have a fifteen-year mortgage with an original loan amount of $100,000, which means a payment of $740 per month. Each mortgage payment is made up of principal and interest and for the first half of the loan's term, the payment is mostly interest.

There is basically three ways to pay off this mortgage:

1. You can pay as you go and follow the amortization provided by the bank. The loan will follow its progression and will ultimately be paid off.
2. You can pay extra money toward the loan to shorten the amortization and reduce the amount of interest paid. By taking approximately a third of your mortgage payment, or $245, and applying it every month toward your loan balance, you will accelerate the payoff by roughly four years. The drawback to this approach is the potential of losing your

interest deduction for tax purposes, and tying your money into your house. Another drawback to paying the principal off early is that banks do not lend money to people who really need it. In other words, if you find yourself without a job, you cannot approach the bank with a request to send back the extra payments you paid them when you had the extra money. In addition, qualifying for a loan to get your extra payments back without a job is unlikely.

3.   You can pay yourself, by taking the money you would otherwise pay toward the mortgage, and instead saving it over the length of the loan until your savings and the loan balance converge, allowing you to pay your loan off in a lump sum. This option also has the advantage of taking money you would have otherwise added to your equity (which we learned earlier would earn a zero percent rate of return) and attempt to earn a rate of return above zero, which can help accelerate the payoff. For example, let's assume that instead of paying off extra principal, you save the same $245 per month at four percent interest. Doing this, you would have enough to pay off your mortgage in ten years, a full year earlier than sending extra money to your bank! Another advantage of this approach is that you can maintain your full tax advantage, while keeping your money liquid. If your life plans were to shift, or you lost your job, you would still have access to your money. One argument you will hear from opponents to this approach is that there is no guarantee of a four precent rate of return on any savings. However, there is no guarantee that your home will appreciate either. So unless you want to play the "what if" game, option three is the most flexible and reliable approach to accelerating a mortgage payoff.

In terms of retirement planning, your home's equity is potentially one of the biggest assets you will have. Yet it is not liquid, and in terms of assets, your property doesn't provide anything other than shelter. Your equity is trapped in the house and is only available if one of two things occurs:

1.   You can sell the home and downsize the cost of the home to keep some of the equity in cash for providing income or other lifestyle needs.

2. You can refinance the home and pull the home's equity out in cash, leaving you with cash in hand and a new mortgage payment.

As I mentioned before, your home is a unique asset, since it provides a home for your family and also acts as an investment for your future. Knowing how to manage your home's equity, and maintaining an informed mindset for how to use the equity, will enable you to make full use of this valuable asset.

CHAPTER FIFTEEN

Social Security

In 1935, President Franklin D. Roosevelt's administration established Social Security to help alleviate poverty resulting from the
Great Depression. When the plan was announced, it was deemed
a "social insurance" program and received a great amount of op-
position for being a form of socialism. Social Security was the
first such program administered by the federal government and
has been a primary source of income for retirees ever since.

Although it is often believed that Social Security will not
be available for future generations, it is unknown whether such
rumors are realistic, due to the trajectory of social programs being issued by our government, which gives every indication that
such programs will continue to grow in the future. With that said,
I believe it is important to know and understand what your benefits are, as well as positioning yourself to take full advantage of
the system that is in place.

Social Security is a retirement asset no different than a pension. In fact, it can arguably be better in many cases, considering
that it is adjusted for inflation, is tax advantaged, is guaranteed
for life, and is backed by the federal government.

The tax advantages of Social Security are worth mentioning
and support the argument for adding more money into tax-free
accounts. When you begin receiving benefits, the portion of your
Social Security income that is subject to federal tax depends on

your income. If your income is below $25,000 as a single tax payer, or $32,000 if married filing jointly, none of your Social Security benefits will be taxed. If your income exceeds this amount, then half of your benefit becomes taxable until you reach $34,000 of income as a single taxpayer, or $44,000 if married, filing jointly. Once your income exceeds this amount, eighty-five percent of your benefits become taxable. In one respect, the fact that you Social Security benefits are never one hundred percent taxed is a good thing but on the other hand it could be argued that you should not be subject to any taxes (up to what you put in) since you contributed to the plan.

If you recall, I mentioned before that you should consider adding more money to tax-free accounts, and this is why. You want to keep your taxable income in retirement as low as possible, to stay below the income threshold, to avoid having to pay tax on your Social Security benefits.

Eligibility for Social Security is based on three factors:

1. Your earnings
2. How long you expect to live
3. When you elect to begin your benefits

Once you reach retirement age, you cannot change your earning history, nor can you know your life expectancy. Therefore, the only factor you have any control over is when you elect to receive your benefits. This is by far the most complex part of Social Security planning and requires a thorough understanding of your options. While the variables are complex, there are opportunities for you, which we will spend some time looking at.

As a single person, Social Security is fairly straightforward. You are eligible for a reduced benefit as early as age sixty-two, and full retirement benefits are available for those born between 1943 and 1954, who retire at age sixty-six. Determining when to begin receiving your benefits is largely impacted by how badly you need to retire before full retirement eligibility, and how long you plan to live to reach a break-even point with your benefits.

For example, if you are age sixty-two and your full retirement benefit is $1,000 per month, your early retirement amount would be $750, or 75% of your full benefit. As mentioned a moment ago, knowing your break-even point is a determining factor for when to begin receiving benefits. If you begin drawing Social

Security at age sixty-two, you would receive $36,000 by age sixty-six. By age seventy, you would have received $72,000, and by seventy-five, $117,000. If you wait to receive your full Social Security benefits at age sixty-six, you would have received $48,000 by age seventy, and $108,000 by the age of seventy-five. Your break-even age would be seventy-eight, with $144,000.

So which option should you take? I can answer that question when you tell me how long you will live.

Most people will elect to take the reduced benefit if they plan to retire at age sixty-two, while people who plan to continue working will usually wait until age sixty-six. The primary reason people will hold off on taking their benefit is that if they plan to continue working, any income they make over allowable limits will see a deduction of one of every two dollars you receive in benefits. This "penalty" discourages early benefits for those who plan to continue working.

The calculations for when to take your Social Security benefits are not as cut and dried for married couples. For a married couple, the same basic rules apply; however, having the ability to receive a spousal benefit makes the calculations more complex.

A husband (or wife) is eligible to receive half of their spouse's benefit once the spouse begins taking their benefit. This enables anyone married eligible to receive Social Security benefits. This would also be used if one spouse makes more money than another, and the spousal benefit is more than what a spouse would receive on his or her own.

It is important to note that only one spouse can elect to receive a spousal benefit because oddly enough, the rules are more favorable for a divorced couple. If you are divorced and were married to your ex for a period of ten or more years, you are eligible to receive a spousal benefit regardless of whether or not your former spouse has elected their benefit. What is unique about the way Social Security is arranged is that two divorced people can both elect to receive spousal benefits while allowing their own benefits to continue to growing (if elected two years prior to full retirement age) while having the ability to switch to their own benefit at age seventy.

Congress made several changes to Social Security in 2015 that took away some privileges previously available. My suggestion is that if you are planning to file for Social Security, give my office a call before making an election to discuss your options.

CHAPTER SIXTEEN

Pension Planning

If you work for the government or are part of a large union, you may very well have a pension or defined benefit plan available to you when you retire. These types of plans have become more antiquated over the years in the private sector, since more affordable options have become available. For the private sector, the high costs associated with administering pension plans have forced many companies to choose voluntary retirement options (such as 401k plans and other defined contribution plans) over defined benefit plans (such as pensions).

It is important to understand that a pension is simply a promise of future benefits, which by definition allows the rules of the savings plan to change or be discontinued at any time, leaving you vulnerable. If you consider that you have no control over the plan itself, and that the trending trajectory of such plans is diminishing, I personally would not rely solely on the promised benefits to provide for your retirement, regardless of how good they are.

With all that said, if you are one of the fortunate few who have a pension, I want to help you make the most of the benefits available to you. These strategies have helped numerous retirees maximize their pensions and help to avoid costly traps that people fall into each and every day.

It is important to keep in mind that since all pensions are not the same, some of what we will discuss in this chapter may not apply to you. Understanding your pension is key to knowing how to maximize the benefits.

Most pensions have a formula that takes into account the number of years you have been working, how much money you have earned, and your age. A combination of these factors typically equates to a predetermined number provided by the pension plan that produces your benefits. These parameters limit who can participate, based on a minimum number of years of service on one end, and a cap on the other to prevent the benefits from getting too large regardless of how many years you work.

There are essentially two options available with most pensions:

1. A lump sum option
2. An annuity payment option

When a pension lump sum option is offered, it usually means that the pension provider is offering you accelerated monthly payments in the form of a lump sum. For instance, if your monthly pension payment is $5,000 per month or $60,000 per year, the pension may offer you a lump sum equivalent to two years of payments or $120,000 in exchange for a revised annuity payment of $4,000 per month.

The pension provider offers this as an option to reduce their exposure long term. The acceptance of this offer does reduce your annuity payment but provides you with a lump sum of cash to use as you see fit. It can be a win/win for both parties provided the offer is mathematically sound, which in some cases it is not. Another point to consider here is that pensions can become insolvent, making an opportunity to receive a pension lump sum very attractive. In other words, it may not be a bad idea to get your cash while you can and accept the pension lump sum if available.

While some plans offer a lump sum coupled with a reduced monthly annuity payment, other plans may only offer an all or nothing option. For example, if you accept the $120,000 lump sum offer, you are accepting the lump sum payment in exchange for future benefits. In other words, that is all you will receive from the pension.

Keep in mind that this is a hypothetical of what is commonly seen and is not representative of all pensions. The point of these illustrations is to provide an explanation of how the math works with the options being offered.

As far as monthly annuity payments are concerned, what I have found is that most plans offer various options, allowing you to choose the payout most suitable for you and your family. The two most common options are the following:

1. A maximum pension option: this option offers a payment to the pension recipient for as long as he is alive. At his death, the payments discontinue.
2. A reduced pension option: this option is a reduced payment to the pension recipient as long as she is alive. At her death, the payments continue to her spouse for as long as the spouse is alive.

For example, your maximum pension payment might be $5,000 per month, while a reduced payment option might be $4,000 per month, with a difference of $1,000 per month. In this scenario, in order for your spouse to continue to receive pension payments after your death, you must give up $1,000 per month for life. (By the way, if you choose to take the maximum benefit, your spouse has to agree to give up the benefit, so don't get any ideas.)

Another component in this example is that many pensions have a COLA (Cost of Living Adjustment) built in. This could be set by the plan up front, or could be declared each year, calculated based on an index such as the CPI (Consumer Price Index). For illustrative purposes, we will assume that the COLA is five percent per year, starting in the second year.

If you analyze the chart below and compare the maximum benefit to the reduced benefit, you will see the compounding effects of the COLA on the benefit.

Year		Maximum	Reduced	Difference
Year	1	$5,000.00	$4,000.00	$1,000.00
Year	2	$5,250.00	$4,200.00	$1,050.00
Year	3	$5,512.50	$4,410.00	$1,102.50
Year	4	$5,788.13	$4,630.50	$1,157.63
Year	5	$6,077.53	$4,862.03	$1,215.51
Year	6	$6,381.41	$5,105.13	$1,276.28
Year	7	$6,700.48	$5,360.38	$1,340.10
Year	8	$7,035.50	$5,628.40	$1,407.10
Year	9	$7,387.28	$5,909.82	$1,477.46
Year	10	$7,756.64	$6,205.31	$1,551.33
Year	11	$8,144.47	$6,515.58	$1,628.89
Year	12	$8,551.70	$6,841.36	$1,710.34
Year	13	$8,979.28	$7,183.43	$1,795.86
Year	14	$9,428.25	$7,542.60	$1,885.65
Year	15	$9,899.66	$7,919.73	$1,979.93
Year	16	$10,394.64	$8,315.71	$2,078.93
Year	17	$10,914.37	$8,731.50	$2,182.87
Year	18	$11,460.09	$9,168.07	$2,292.02
Year	19	$12,033.10	$9,626.48	$2,406.62
Year	20	$12,634.75	$10,107.80	$2,526.95

Over twenty years, the maximum benefit grows to a whopping $12,634.75 per month, while the reduced benefit grows to $10,107.80 per month. That is a monthly difference of $2,526.95 per month! Multiply this by twelve months and you find that the annual difference in payments in year twenty is $33,065.95. If you combine the difference of all twenty years, you will find that the benefit difference is $396,791.45.

So what did we learn from this chart? We learned that the price of extending a benefit to your spouse after you die is $396,791. Essentially you are paying the pension provider $396,791 to offer your spouse a benefit after you die. Keep in mind that this assumes you die in the twentieth year. If you live ten or twenty more years, these benefits and costs continue to grow larger.

To look at this even more closely, when you think about it, if you are paying a premium each year for someone to provide a benefit to your spouse when you die, you are essentially buying life insurance, aren't you? Not only are you buying a life insurance policy, you are buying a very expensive policy.

Here is another thing to consider if you are thinking of buying the insurance through your pension versus buying it from an insurance company. If you buy the insurance through the pension, this benefit is only transferable to your surviving spouse. If you have children and you and your spouse both happen to die in a car crash, the benefits do not transfer to your heirs.

So let's review what we know so far:

- The cost of the policy goes up each year, since the COLA received on the maximum benefit is greater than what is received on the reduced benefit. The chasm between the two benefit totals continues to widen over time.
- The benefit continues to go down since each year you and your spouse are both aging, making the number of years the benefit may be received less each year that passes.
- You disinherit your family, since the benefits are not transferrable to your heirs.

Now let's move on.

Let me ask you a question: considering that the pension plan has to offer this option to all plan participants, and an insurance company has the option to only insure healthy individuals, is it conceivable that a healthy person could purchase a life insurance policy from an insurance company more cheaply?

If the insurance is bought through the pension plan, on average you will have paid $20,831 per year to purchase this life insurance. If the policy is bought more straightforwardly using a life insurance company, your premiums could have been considerably less. (I hesitate to give a premium here because it would depend on your age, gender, and health, but it is conceivable that the premium would be twenty to twenty-five percent cheaper.)

Over the years, I have studied the different aspects of this and have discovered that when the reduced benefit is chosen, not only are you paying an exorbitant premium for a declining benefit, you are also potentially disinheriting your family. Once you and your spouse are deceased, there is nothing left to pass on and all the premiums and costs associated with all these benefits die with you.

The exception to this example is if you are not healthy, making it difficult to get coverage with an insurance company. In this scenario, the only logical option is to accept the insurance provided by the pension plan. And of course, if you are single, then much of this is a non-issue, and you would clearly take the maximum benefit.

As with all the topics discussed in this book, I want to provide you with filters to help you make the best decision and choose the best option for your situation. Many books and "experts" will attempt to give a one-size-fits-all recommendation for a specific topic. Unfortunately, while that kind of black and white advice may be good for some, it may not be good for others. So I want to provide you with the tools and the insight I use each and every day to help you create a mindset of how to best approach each topic. I hope my approach is working for you as you continue onto the next chapter. If you have questions at any point throughout this book, please feel free to email me your questions at yourmoney@sfgplan.com.

— CHAPTER SEVENTEEN —

Charitable Giving

For many of us, charitable giving is driven by an inherent desire to be a part of something bigger than ourselves. The act of giving makes us feel like we are making a difference in our community and impacting others in a positive way. A donation to a church, sponsoring a child's sports team, building a community center, or a forming a foundation allows us to leave a fingerprint on the next generation.

Regardless of what drives you to give, understanding your options for how to give is a vital part of making the most significant impact. While a cash donation is the most common form of giving and is the easiest way to contribute to your favorite charity, there are other ways to give that can provide significant funding for the beneficiary.

In an earlier chapter, we discussed life insurance for financial planning strategies, but as time goes by, your need for insurance coverage may reduce or even diminish, for example, after the kids are raised and retirement approaches. There may come a time when you find yourself kicking around the idea of canceling the contract, since the original need for the policy is no longer present. If this is you, you might want to think about reestablishing its purpose instead of cashing it in. The versatility of life insurance makes the contract a tremendous vehicle for philanthropic purposes. You can donate the policy to your church by simply changing the ownership and beneficiary of the contract, and at your death, the institution receives the death benefit.

Another approach to using life insurance for charitable purposes is redirecting money you plan to give outright to the charity to purchase a life insurance policy. By taking a lump sum of cash and purchasing a life policy that could double or triple the amount the charity receives through death benefit proceeds.

If you have highly appreciated assets such as real estate or stocks, you may consider using these assets to donate to your charity of choice. The capital gain taxes can be avoided, and the asset becomes a tax deduction if used as a charitable contribution. If you need the income from the asset but would ultimately like to give it to charity, you may want to consider a charitable remainder trust (CRT). This type of trust is an alternative for people who want to make a substantial gift to a charitable organization but would like to maintain control over the asset while they are still living.

A CRT is an irrevocable trust. This means that once it is set up and a charitable gift is made, it cannot be undone. In order to realize its full potential, a CRT requires special legal, accounting, and tax administration. Gifts to a CRT can be made in cash, but more often consist of highly appreciated stock, real estate, or a closely held business interest. Some of the benefits of a CRT are that it does the following:

- Provides a current income tax deduction
- Defers capital gains taxes
- Reduces or eliminates estate taxes
- Provides an income stream, often for life
- Benefits the charity of your choice

The flip side to a charitable trust is that if you place an asset into the trust, you are technically removing it from your estate. In other words, the charity of choice becomes the beneficiary of the asset and removes it from your heir's inheritance. Often this is a quandary that is easily solved by setting up a wealth-replacement strategy. This strategy is designed to replace the value of the asset with a life insurance policy that has a death benefit equal to the value.

Since the primary financial purpose for making a charitable donation is the tax savings, adding a wealth replacement strategy can create pools of money that would not otherwise exist, or would have otherwise gone to Uncle Sam. By taking some of your tax savings resulting from the CRT and redirecting it to a wealth replacement strategy, you can purchase a life insurance policy that allows for proceeds to pass to your beneficiaries without any income taxes. The charity receives a donation, your heirs receive a tax-free inheritance, and you receive a sizable tax deduction.

One other giving strategy is through a charitable gift annuity. This type of gift is an agreement between a donor and the charity where the donor makes an irrevocable gift to the charity. In exchange for the gift, the charity agrees to pay an income back to the donor for life.

The gift annuity transaction is not fully deductible, but it does provide a tax deduction for the donor. The arrangement is in part a gift to charity and in part the purchase of an annuity.

A charitable gift annuity offers several benefits to the donor:

- It provides an immediate income tax deduction to the donor.
- It pays a lifetime income to one or two individuals, part of which is federal income tax-free.
- The income payout from the gift annuity can begin immediately or can be deferred until some future start date.
- The transferred assets are removed from donor's gross estate for federal estate tax purposes.

If charitable giving is part of your financial plan each year, then hopefully these ideas have motivated you to consider other more significant ways to give. If you have not made giving a part of your life but would like to begin, here are four things to do to get yourself started:

1. Determine what you want. Think about and create a personal wish list of what you want to give to. Identify key financial goals you want to fulfill with the donation and write them down with as many details as possible to give yourself a clear image of what you want.
2. Visualize how you want to be remembered. Think about how you want to be remembered and what impact you want to make on the next generation of your family and community.

Having a clear written down vision for what you want is the first step to fulfilling any goal.

3. Take an inventory. Think about and write down what you own such as stocks, bonds, land, IRAs, CDs, life insurance, and any other form of asset that you may have. Then make a list of debt obligations and necessary purchases. This will help you to better identify where you are in relationship to your goals and what resources you have available.

4. Take action. Now that you have a clear picture of what you have and what you want, the next step is to put your plan into action. Make charitable giving part of your monthly budget and financial plan. A well-thought-out and properly arranged plan increases the likelihood of success.

CHAPTER EIGHTEEN

Estate Planning

It is said that there are two certainties in life: death and taxes. Although this is a cliché, we know it to be true. All wage earners know their responsibility for filing and paying their taxes. We all know the routine of getting applicable receipts together, gathering 1099s and W-2s and preparing those dreaded IRS forms. Some people file their tax forms early to get the tax refund they have anxiously anticipated, while others wait until the day taxes are due to get started. Regardless of your approach, you know that the IRS sets a strict deadline for when you must have our completed forms in the mail to avoid penalties.

While tax processes and deadlines are fairly black and white, the death part of the cliché is not so predictable. We do not know when this deadline will hit, making those who wait until the last minute...well, late. If we assume our death will be from natural causes, we can narrow it down to maybe a twenty-year time frame. However, there is no guarantee about how much time we have left on this Earth, making it very difficult to know how long we have to get ready.

What I have found is that the vast majority of people do not have any legal work prepared to communicate their wishes to family and friends once they are gone. I am not sure why this is, but I do know that when I ask whether or not someone has legal work prepared, the answer is often the same: no, he does not have any legal work, but yes, he knows that he needs to get it done. I am not in the business of trying to understand why people do what they do. All I can do is work off the assumption that the reason people put off getting their affairs in order is that the "deadline" of when this legal work will be needed is too far into the future. When we look at estate planning, it is best to assume you will die tomorrow.

One thing we know is that it is our responsibility to take the necessary steps to make sure our affairs are in order, and that our plans for our children are clear. Some key questions to ask yourself when it comes to financial planning are these:

- Who will take care of your children while they are still minors?
- Who will handle the financial affairs for your children if they are minors?
- If your child has special needs, how will those be satisfied, since such children can often require a lifetime of care?
- If you are in a second marriage and you, your new spouse, or both have children from another marriage, how will your assets be divided, and who will distribute the assets?
- What happens if you, your spouse, or both suffer an illness, or have an accident that leaves you unable to function? Who will take care of your financial affairs while you are still living?
- What happens if you, your spouse, or both suffer an illness or have an accident that leaves you on life support? Who will make the decision about "pulling the plug"?

I am not an attorney, but I am quite certain that there are other considerations for planning your estate. However, my point for providing this information is not to offer a substitute for professional legal advice but to help you understand that there are many important considerations, making a case for why you should have legal work in place.

One of the most popular questions I get from clients is about the difference between a will and a trust. The way I answer the question is by explaining the following:

- A will is a document that expresses your wishes to the probate courts for how your children will be cared for and how your assets will be distributed at death.
- A trust is like a box into which you place things. Once a trust is established, you can transfer your home, investments, and other assets into the trust. A trust bypasses probate altogether and can immediately enforce your wishes for your children and your assets.

What is important to note is that without some form of legal work in place, most states have a process to make these childcare and asset distribution decisions for you. These decisions more than likely will not match what you would want done if something were to happen to you or your spouse, and this is another reason to get this completed.

We have covered the need for legal work in the event of a death, but there are a couple of other considerations that most attorneys include in your planning.

- A financial power of attorney is a legal document that allows someone to act on your behalf if you are incapacitated. The paying of bills or conducting day-to-day business requires someone to have the legal ability to write checks and execute transactions.
- A medical power of attorney is a document that contains the details for your medical-related wishes. If you were to become incapacitated, unable to make medical decisions for yourself, this document informs the medical caregivers how you want to be cared for. Otherwise, your family and the caregivers are left to debate what the best course of action is for you.

As with everything I have discussed in this book, the knowledge of what needs to be taken care of is the first step in getting it done. Make sure your legal affairs are up to date and reflect your wishes.

CHAPTER NINETEEN

Choosing a Professional

A few years ago, I was seeking medical advice and needed to find a specialist for the type of procedure I needed to have done. I began my search with a referral from my primary doctor who sent me to a doctor in his building. The appointment was set, and a few weeks later I had a chance to sit down with him to begin talking about the procedure.

After my visit, I realized that my only filter for hiring a doctor was my gut. In other words, I was feeling around in the dark, seeking a good feeling or a bad feeling about what to do, while not knowing what to even ask or look for when hiring this doctor, who would be operating on me.

That is when I realized that this is EXACTLY the experience people have when they are venturing out to hire a financial professional. They are forced to make important decisions about their money with nothing more than their gut instincts, and I knew through my own experience with hiring a doctor that I needed to get the word out about what to look for in a financial professional.

Unfortunately, not all professionals have red flags waving in front of you, warning you of a problem. Many advisors are good salesman and even use a large company name to lend themselves credibility.

So I would like to share with you the questions I would ask another financial professional if I were to interview her. After you have asked a few of the right questions, your interaction with her, coupled with the knowledge of what the professional can do for you, will help you make a well-informed decision. These points are in no particular order, and all carry a certain level of importance. Here we go!

1. Is this person a fiduciary?

A fiduciary is required by law to act in the best interest of the client. Contrary to what most people believe or understand, the financial advisor they are working with may be working more for the company she works for, rather than in your best interest. Ask her whom she is working for.

2. How long has he been in business?

There is a revolving door in the finance business, and considering that there are plenty of investment professionals who have a proven track record, with more than twenty years in the business, there is no need to settle for an advisor with little experience. Ask him why you should work with him over someone with more experience.

3. How does she get paid?

There are two general methods for how a financial advisor gets paid: one is through commissions, and the other is from fees. There are many opinions about how an advisor should get paid for her services. Having an advisor who can work with you under either arrangement may offer you more options from which you can negotiate. Ask her if she can work through both commissions and fees.

4. Does he work for himself or for someone else?

There are many financial professionals who are hired by a company to sell their products, and who are given a title of financial advisor. If the person you are working with does not have ownership or decision-making abilities at a corporate level, he may not have the flexibility to offer the full range of products and services you may need. Ask him if he owns the business advertised on his door.

5. Does she have a network of other professionals?

Financial advising is more than picking a few stocks and bonds. It is more about financial planning and the coordination of professional services such as insurance, mortgage, estate planning, tax, and investments. There is direct correlation among most of these areas, which can have an overlapping effect on other areas of your money. If the financial professional is only interested in helping you with your investments, you may want to find someone who has your entire financial picture in mind. Ask specifically whom she will use to offer these services, and how long she has been working with these other professionals.

6. How often does he meet with his clients, and whom do you call when you have a question?

It is fairly easy to get the attention of a financial advisor during the initial contact, but how easy will it be after you become a client? Ideally, you would visit with your advisor annually, to review where you are and evaluate how things are going. In addition, a successful financial advisor spends his days meeting with clients and is not always readily available. So a client service support team is a vitally important part of the quality of service you will receive. Ask for details about what you can expect from the advisor's follow up and client service.

7. What is her investment philosophy?

There are many investments available and picking which is best for you can be a difficult task. Make sure your advisor can offer a wide range of products (from CDs to stocks) and multiple asset classes (from US stocks to commodities) to help create a well-diversified portfolio. Ask her why she is choosing the investments she is choosing, and how they correlate with one another. You may be (unpleasantly) surprised to find out that she is not picking anything specifically for you, but is rather working from a list of products her corporate office has asked her to sell.

8. What will he do to keep you informed between appointments?

What I have found with many financial advisors is that their process for keeping you informed amounts to you receiving a statement from a product company. In this age of social media and email, your financial advisor should be communicating with his clients as a whole every day. Knowledge of what is affecting the markets is important to help you keep your emotions in check, and knowing that your advisor has his finger on the financial pulse of the world can also provide you with a level of confidence. Ask your potential advisor about email frequency, and ascertain whether he has offered any recent seminars that, as a client, you would have been invited to.

So there you have it. These are the eight things I recommend that you find out about your financial advisor. There is significant variation among financial advisors, and I believe that these eight questions will assist you in finding a financial advisor who is right for you.

CHAPTER TWENTY

...Still Want More?

As we have learned throughout this book, your financial decisions must be based on your unique situation and focused on what is most appropriate to help you meet your goals. I often say that financial products and services are similar to medical prescriptions and procedures: there are many to choose from, but just because one prescription or procedure is considered great does not mean everyone should take it. The same is true for financial planning. There are many good products and strategies available, but it does not mean you should necessarily do them. They need to be right for you.

What I want to do in this chapter is provide some simple answers to some of the most common questions about money.

Investment Options

For many people, mutual funds or ETFs are going to be the easiest and most cost-effective investment option. All you need to decide is what you are trying to accomplish through your investment. If you want your money to create an income, choose an income fund. If you want your money to have long-term aggressive growth, choose an aggressive growth fund. If you want to invest in China, consider an international fund. I have obviously simplified this, but for the purpose of what we are discussing, it really is that simple.

International investing entails special risk considerations, including currency fluctuations, lower liquidity, economic and political risks, and differences in accounting methods. Past performance cannot guarantee future results.

Individual stocks and bonds I feel are much more complicated and risky choices. For the average investor, this is an option I would stay away from unless you choose an account that is managed by a professional, for a fee. The advantage of a managed account is that unlike a mutual fund, you actually own the securities within the account, which offers strategic tax advantages. A fee-based account is advantageous since by nature, the account is actively traded, which means that the securities are being purchased and sold on a regular basis. If you use a commission-based account, you are being charged for each transaction. In a managed account, you are not paying transaction fees for the trades, but you do pay a percentage for the advice.

Annuity Options

Should you buy an annuity? Maybe. My opinion of the use of annuities differs from that of most financial advisors. Fundamentally, an annuity is tax-favorable by design, which means money deposited into the contract, though not deductible, does offer tax-deferred growth. In other words, your money grows without annual tax obligations, but defers the tax for when you withdraw money from the contract. However, I do not recommend using annuities for this purpose. The fees are higher than more traditional investments, and the earnings are taxed as ordinary income versus capital gains, as with other investments.

The "maybe" comes into play when you consider all the income options available with annuities. There are guarantees offered by annuities that are not available within other traditional investments. As we have discussed in previous chapters, qualified money such as IRAs and 401ks, are typically used for income purposes and are tax-favored by nature. So using an annuity for qualified money goes against the inherent design of the contracts, which is tax-deferred growth. Rather you would use it to take advantages of their guarantees (for a fee of course). For more information about this, you can go to my website at www.skrobonjafinancialgroup.com.

Life Insurance Options

In the majority of situations, term insurance will be the most economical and suitable option. A twenty- to thirty-year term policy will cover most liabilities and responsibilities. Often life insurance is needed to provide for dependent children or to cover a mortgage liability, making a twenty- or thirty-year policy adequate.

There are a few exceptions to this, one of which is relating to pension-planning, as we covered in a previous chapter. In this scenario, the need for coverage is ongoing, up till the day you die. You are protecting an income for your spouse at your death. Therefore, the insurance coverage by design must last as long as you do. A term policy cannot fulfill this obligation.

A second scenario where term insurance may not be the best fit is for higher income individuals who have been excluded through our tax code from participating in tax-favored accounts such as Roth IRAs, and who have a need for life insurance. Often these individuals have maxed out their 401k or retirement plan options and have a desire to save more money on a tax-favored basis. In situations such as this, a cash-value life insurance policy may make sense if the contract is designed properly.

Whole life insurance tends to gain in popularity when the interest rate environment is low, and people are seeking higher yields on their money. This type of coverage is often used to hold large amounts of cash for specific future uses, such as the purchase of an automobile, or funding a child's college tuition. The reason behind the attractiveness of such a life policy is that this type of life insurance offers a higher long-term rate of return than most other low-risk investments, without the market risk. In addition, with life insurance's favorable loan provisions, accessing money from the policy allows for tax-free loans, along with its unique dividend structure where the amount of money you borrow from the contract does not affect the dividend growth of the cash value of the policy. You can refer back to chapter nine for the details of how this works. You just need to keep in mind that for this strategy to work you have to use specially designed contracts, and they must be set up and funded correctly. If you have questions or would like to learn more about your options, call my office at 636-296-5225 or email me at yourmoney@sfgplan.com.

Mortgage Refinance Options

One way to determine whether or not to refinance is by calculating the math of the transaction. In other words, what are you gaining by paying the fees? A simple rule of thumb is that if by reducing your payment, you can make up the cost of the loan within eighteen to twenty-four months, then it may make sense. In other words, if your cost is $2,000 and you are saving $100 per month in your payments, then you will break even on the transaction in twenty months. Although this is not the only consideration, it is where I would start.

However, it is not always about the transaction itself. If you have equity in your home and plan to make home improvements, I tend to lean towards using your home's equity to fund the project. In other words, have the home pay for its own improvements. In this case, you should look at the potential appreciation of the home's value resulting from the improvements against the cost of the loan. You can also refer to the chapter on home equity, which provides insight into using your home's equity.

— CHAPTER TWENTY-ONE —

Q & A

I have covered the most important aspects of financial planning in this book. Hopefully, you have found a new way of thinking about money and have a newfound confidence about what you can achieve, if you take the time to do the right things at the right time.

It is likely that perhaps you still have specific questions that I was not able to answer in this book. Therefore, I wanted to give you a chapter dedicated to the top questions I get on a regular basis and attempt to answer them in a general context.

Should I buy gold?

My answer to this question is always the same: it depends. It depends on why you want to buy it. If you want to purchase gold (or silver) for long-term appreciation then I would say no. If you want to purchase the precious metal to offset a depreciating dollar or other economic concerns, then I would say yes. So, as you can see, it depends.

Should I contribute to my 401k?

Yes, you should, up to what your employer matches, unless you are single, approaching retirement, and have already maxed out a Roth IRA. Then I would say max it out.

Should I pay my home off?

If it is keeping you up at night then yes. If you want to make an educated financial decision with your money then reread my chapter on Home Equity.

Do I need more life insurance?

This obviously depends. A rule of thumb is to have 10-20x your income in life insurance coverage. If you are single with no obligations then perhaps you do not need very much but if you are married with young children then you should consider the upper extreme to cover your financial obligations for your family.

Should I invest or pay off my debt first?

I would have to say that you need to focus on debt reduction (excluding your home). It does not make much sense to invest at an unpredictable rate when you are paying debt interest of five to ten percent or more.

How much money should I have in emergency savings?

A rule of thumb is to have three to six months of your budget needs in savings. If you lose a job or something unforeseen occurs you will be well equipped to handle the set back.

Where should I put my money for big-ticket purchases or short-term savings?

As I discussed in chapter nine, a Specially Designed Life Insurance (SDLI) program is a possibility for the right person and situation. This approach takes discipline and there are limitations but could be a viable option as a banking alternative. Refer back to chapter nine to learn how this strategy works.

Should I reduce the amount of tax I am having withheld in my check?

If you historically receive a tax refund as a result of filing your taxes, what is happening is that the IRS is sending back to you the money you loaned them for the last tax year with zero interest. That means each time you received a paycheck, a portion of your money was voluntarily sent to the IRS which they did not ask for. If you had to physically write this check, my guess would be that you could find a better place to send extra money other than to the IRS. Reduce it.

Should I take my money out of the stock market?

If you know and understand anything about the market you know that it goes up and down. Trying to time when to get in and out of the market is a losing proposition because nobody knows when it will go up or down to a point when it would absolutely make sense to do one or the other. If you are investing, ride out the volatility until you need the money. *Investment in stocks will fluctuate with changes in market conditions.*

Should I roll over my 401k from my previous employer?

Something to keep in mind when making the decision to leave your money behind is that the 401k plan itself gives your employer fiduciary control over the retirement assets in the plan. In other words, your employer makes decisions on your behalf about what investment options are available. Many investors choose to establish more control over the management of their retirement assets by rolling money into an Individual Retirement Account. This transfer of money away from the employer can allow you more flexibility and gives you the ability to make your own investment decisions. As with any investment decision, there is likely cost involved which you should consider before making a decision to roll money over.

Should I use a 529 Plan for my children's education fund?

You can. A 529 Plan can be a solid tax play for a state income tax advantage, but it does come with some strings attached that you should be aware of. Since there is really no way to know what the tuition bill will be until your child picks a college and all of the available scholarships are calculated, you are shooting in the dark when determining how much money you need to save in the plan. You could end up having too much money tied up in the plan. In addition, there are other ancillary variables that come into play when it comes to saving for your child's future. What if he chooses to not go to college? What if there is a greater need for a vehicle when the time comes to use the money? The more flexible approach to saving for a child's education is to use an UGMA or UTMA. There are no tax benefits, but they are more flexible. You have to decide for yourself which is more important: flexibility or tax benefits. *An investor should consider the investment objectives, risks, charges and expenses associated with 529 plans before investing. More information about municipal fund securities is available in the issuer's official statement. The official statement should be read carefully before investing. Most states offer their own 529 programs which may provide advantages and benefits exclusively for their residents and taxpayers. The tax implications of a 529 plan should be discussed with a qualified tax advisor.*

How do you know what to invest in?

There are many "good" investment options available, but much like prescription medications, they should not be used unless there is a diagnosis supporting their use. To know what investments are best for a particular situation, you need to have information, experience, and an understanding of how the product works. Otherwise, you may find yourself using the incorrect investment vehicle, which can be a costly mistake. You can call my office at 636-296-5225, and begin the process of finding the option most suitable for your situation.

What is the most popular product retirees use for their retirement fund?

In my experience it has been an annuity. The guarantees associated with certain annuities make it a desirable option for someone wanting to protect her money. There are many different types of programs which can satisfy most individual preferences, too many to get into here. You can refer to the chapter on investment options, or contact my office at 636-296-5225, or email me at yourmoney@sfgplan.com.

How do you feel about individual stocks?

I am not a day trader, so I tend to leave the trading to someone who has the time to research when to buy and sell. I am not completely opposed to them, but I prefer ETFs and mutual funds. They are more widely diversified and actively managed.

Should I carry disability insurance?

Yes, otherwise you will be dependent on the government, and taxpayers will be responsible for caring for you financially. Take responsibility, and purchase the coverage.

How do I obtain information about my Social Security benefits, since they no longer mail the information to my home?

You can visit the Social Security Administration's website and use their online calculator to get the information you are seeking: http://www.ssa.gov/retire2/AnypiaApplet.html.

— CHAPTER TWENTY-TWO —

Conclusion

Congratulations! You have broken through to the other side of financial- and retirement- planning literacy. I am honored that you have welcomed me into your life, by allowing me to share my decades of real-life experience working with people just like you. What I've presented here are strategies I continue to use each and every day to help my clients find financial congruence in their life. It is my hope that this book can help you discover a new way of thinking about money that will allow you to attain the results you desire and deserve in your life.

The knowledge you have used to get to where you are today may also be what keeps you where you are right now. I am confident that you now have the tools and information to understand that getting to the next level financially, and achieving real, lasting results, involves adopting new ways of thinking, feeling, and acting. It also involves adopting new resources, asking new questions, and putting yourself into a new position for growth.

However, simply reading a book is not enough. You have to take action for change to occur. Regardless of whether you are just starting out, or whether you have already accumulated wealth, there is always a next level to reach, and I want to help you get there.

Whether you are focused on retirement income, a specific investment, or a financial-planning goal, your next step is to define with crystal clarity the results you want to achieve. Once you decide to reach that next level financially, then it is time to find a quality financial professional to assist you with your financial planning needs. To learn how my team can work with you, give my office a call at 636-296-5225.

Thanks for reading!

---

prospectus. Investors should consider their investment objectives and risks, along with the product's charges and expenses before investing. Please read the prospectus carefully before investing.

Annuity contracts contain exclusions, limitations, reductions of benefits and terms for keeping them in force. Investors should consider the contract and the underlying portfolios' investment objectives, risks, and charges and expenses carefully before investing. Please read the annuity prospectus for more complete information, including all charges and expenses before investing or sending money.

This material should not be considered a solicitation of an offer to sell/ buy any specific security or offering. Investors are advised to consider the investment objective, risks, charges and expenses of an offering carefully before investing.

A policy change may incur fees and costs, and may also require a medical examination. This scenario is for illustrative purposes only and does not represent an actual client. Results may vary. Any descriptions involving life insurance policies and its use as an alternative form of financing or risk management techniques are provided for illustration purposes only, will not apply in all situations, may not be fully indicative of any present or future investments, and may be changed at the discretion of the insurance carrier, General Partner and/or Manager and are not intended to reflect guarantees on securities performance. The term private banking alternatives or specially designed life insurance contracts (SDLIC) is not meant to insinuate that the issuer is creating a real bank for its clients or communicating that life insurance companies are the same as traditional banking institutions. This material is educational in nature and should not be deemed as a solicitation of any specific product or service. All investments involve risk and a potential loss of principal. Kalos Capital nor Kalos Management offer tax and legal advice. Please consult with a tax advisor or attorney for advice regarding the impact on your portfolio.

Made in the USA
Monee, IL
28 December 2021

87421149R00075